CRITICAL PERSPECTIVES ON
SEXUAL HARASSMENT
AND
GENDER VIOLENCE

ANALYZING THE ISSUES

CRITICAL PERSPECTIVES ON
SEXUAL HARASSMENT
AND
GENDER VIOLENCE

Edited by Bridey Heing

Enslow Publishing

101 W. 23rd Street
Suite 240
New York, NY 10011
USA

Published in 2018 by Enslow Publishing, LLC
101 W. 23rd Street, Suite 240, New York, NY 10011

Library of Congress Cataloging-in-Publication Data

Names: Heing, Bridey, editor.
Title: Critical perspectives on sexual harassment and gender violence / edited by Bridey Heing.
Description: New York : Enslow Publishing, [2018] | Series: Analyzing the issues | Audience: Grades 7-12. | Includes bibliographical references and index.
Identifiers: LCCN 2017015648 | ISBN 9780766091665 (library bound) | ISBN 9780766095625 (paperback)
Subjects: LCSH: Sexual harassment of women. | Women — Violence against.
Classification: LCC HQ1237 .C75 2017 | DDC 305.42 — dc23
LC record available at https://lccn.loc.gov/2017015648

Printed in China

CONTENTS

INTRODUCTION

For millions of women around the world, sexual harassment and gender violence are a part of everyday life. From catcalls to sexual assault, actions taken against women based on their gender have shaped the way women engage with society and public spaces. Although sexual harassment and gender violence may seem worlds apart, they are part of the same spectrum of treatment that has been shown to or used against women for centuries. These issues have also generated widespread debate about how best to protect women, who must take responsibility for these actions, and whether it is fair to treat violence against men and women differently in a modern society.

"Sexual harassment" is a term that came into use in 1975, although it was taking place long before then. It refers to any unwanted sexual advance or remark made in a professional or social setting, and it was extremely common as women moved into the workforce in the late nineteenth and early twentieth centuries. In 1976, *Redbook* magazine ran a survey that found 80 percent of respondents had experienced a form of sexual harassment at work, which can range from unwanted touching to inappropriate remarks. According to the US Equal Employment Opportunity Commission, 12,860 allegations were filed with them in 2016—but many believe that the number of actual sexual harassment cases is much higher.[1]

Gender violence refers to acts of physical violence against someone based on their gender, including rape, assault, or the threat of such acts. It can also refer to psychological mistreatment, including depriving an individual of full freedom of movement. Gender violence can be carried out by men and women, and the victims can be male or female. But women are disproportionately the victims of gender violence crimes; one in three women are victims of domestic violence while one in four men are, and women are at the highest risk of sexual assault.[2]

Sexual harassment and gender violence both have a large impact on the lives of women. These issues are truly global in scale, as women from every country on Earth experience some level of both harassment and gender violence. Those experiencing sexual harassment may come to see their workspace as unsafe, which could lead them to quit. Sexual harassment can also make it difficult for women to be promoted or presented with opportunities they deserve. Gender violence, which is sometimes used as a weapon of war, can hinder when and where women are able to travel, force them to flee their homes, or leave lasting emotional and physical trauma.

While the impact of sexual harassment and gender violence is very real, there is still a great deal of debate about what the terms encompass and how best to confront both issues. There are many laws around the world that govern sexual harassment and gender violence, yet both remain common globally. One issue is a lack of proper handling of cases. According to the Rape, Abuse & Incest National Network (RAINN), an estimated 344 of every 1,000 cases of sexual assault are reported to the police, and an even smaller percentage of those cases are prosecuted.[3] In extreme cases of gender violence, including in cases of war, it can be difficult to bring individuals who carried out those actions to justice. While some feel the best way to combat sexual harassment and gender violence is to properly educate women on how to defend themselves, others feel the responsibility falls on perpetrators, who should be taught to not carry out these actions.

In this book, we'll hear from politicians who have pushed forward legislation against sexual harassment, victims of gender violence, and concerned citizens eager to find ways to better protect those at risk. We'll learn about legal protections, court cases that have shaped our understanding of these issues, and the changing way we as a culture talk about harassment and assault. When taken together, the voices in this collection will show the range of opinions, practices, and impacts of sexual harassment and gender violence on women in the United States and around the world.

CHAPTER 1

WHAT ACADEMICS, EXPERTS, AND RESEARCHERS SAY

Research into sexual harassment and gender violence covers a large number of topics, including psychology, economics, history, and statistics. Experts are able to connect the threads between these many intersecting topics in a way that the media or the average citizen cannot, which gives us a deeper understanding of what causes gender violence and how sexual harassment impacts society. It is impossible to understand the entirety of gender-based discrimination and violence in the context of only one country, so the research shown here draws from findings around the world. Gender violence and harassment emerges in different ways in countries experiencing conflict or instability than in stable states. In these places there are differing impacts and root causes. It is also important to study the effects of projects and initiatives aimed at limiting or stopping harassment and gender violence to understand their successes and failures in crafting future policies. When it comes to fully understanding these topics, research is the critical first step in doing so.

EXCERPT FROM "THE WORLD DEVELOPMENT REPORT GENDER BACKGROUND PAPER" BY SANAM NARAGHI ANDERLINI, FROM THE WORLD BANK, FEBRUARY 19, 2010

PART I: GENDER AS A FACTOR IN EMERGING AND INTERRELATED FORMS OF VIOLENCE

Research in developed and development settings reveals linkages between experiences of violence in the domestic setting and aggressive or violent behavior in the public setting. As discussed below much of the existing information pertains to countries emerging from conflict, where at war's end, the violence continues in new forms, often in the domestic settings. But if conflict and violence prevention practices are to improve, understanding the links between form of violence against women – direct individual and structural – and corporal punishment of children and communal or public violence in non-conflict and pre-conflict settings is also needed.

This section reflects on the linkages between different forms of violence in non-conflict states, conflict situations and post conflict settings. Where available it also points to the data and research that has shaped the discourse, policy and programmatic responses to date.

I.1 GENDER INEQUALITY & DOMESTIC VIOLENCE AS INDICATORS OF PUBLIC VIOLENCE:

I.1.i Gender inequality as a variable or indicator of state-level security and propensity for violence: Using aggregate data from 1954-94, (Caprioli and Boyer 2001, Caprioli 2003) demonstrate that states with higher levels of social, political, economic and gender equality are less likely to rely on military force to settle disputes. They also demonstrate that a higher percentage of women in leadership positions correlates with lower levels of violence.

A more recent study (Hudson et al 2009) compares the efficacy of gender inequality as predictor of instability/ violence compared to other criteria (e.g. level of democracy, Islamic nature of society). Preliminary conclusions of the study demonstrate that the physical security of women is a strong predictor of the peacefulness of a state.

USAID also uses male-female life expectancy ratios at birth as an indicator for state fragility. The rationale given is that good health is an indication of human development and necessary for economic growth. "In every country with a high level of human development, females have longer life expectancy than males, often by five years or more. Thus, in countries with greater gender equity, the ratio is greater than one. In many developing countries, however, the relationship is reversed and the gender ratio is less than one. This a clear sign of serious disadvantages faced by women in obtaining health care, economic opportunities, and social empowerment." (USAID 2006)

Viewed with a lens of conflict or violence prevention, the studies suggest that higher levels of gender equality and women's physical security are not only important indicators of general stability, peacefulness, but that reduction in inequality and improvements to women's security are necessary conditions for stability and economic growth. This mirrors much of the qualitative and empirical work on gendered early warning indicators

(Piza-Lopez & Schmiedl 2000, Moser/UNIFEM 2005) that claim the deterioration in women's security and increases in gender disparity are among the earliest signs of crisis and violence. In effect women are the proverbial canaries in the mine. Being the most susceptible and vulnerable sector of many societies, they are often the first to experience new threats to security – be it from extremist ideologues such as the Taliban, or the growth of organized crime such as human sex traffickers.

I.1.ii Why Tackling Domestic Violence Matters:

Do higher levels of domestic violence pose a threat to communal peace and security? Given the high rates of domestic violence in many countries, the short answer is likely to be 'not directly'. However, qualitative and empirical studies conducted in the US (and other developed countries) do point to linkage and a continuum of violence between the domestic and the public sphere, particularly in terms of the trajectory of individuals' lives – i.e. those most likely to become the foot soldiers and perpetrators of violence. High and rising rates of domestic violence are also tied to increased socio-economic and political stresses and can be indicative of more violence-prone countries and settings.

First, exposure to domestic violence or childhood abuse can lead to aggressive adult behavior. In a 1996 US study 70% of male perpetrators of violence had been victims of childhood abuse (Lisak, Hopper and Song 1996). In a 2009 study Jordanian university students, when comparing their community, media, school or university settings, ranked the family first as the institution contributing to acquiring violent behavior (Okour, Hijazi 2009). A 2006 study of Colombian adolescents also found 'maltreatment' or harsh parenting as directly correlated with violent behavior (Mejia et al 2006). Childhood violence can also affect emotional, cognitive and longer term development (Edleson 1999).

Empirical and longitudinal studies in the US and across cultures indicate that contextual factors in early childhood (e.g. poverty) are indirectly linked to violence but more mediated variables – e.g. changes in family circumstance or disruption in discipline – are more directly linked.[ii] Learnt behavior particularly in terms of how conflict is managed is also more directly correlated. Where higher levels of antisocial or coercive measures are used to resolve conflict, there is an increase in the antisocial aggressive behavior of the child. The correlation between trivial antisocial behavior (e.g. lying, cheating, threatening) and more aggressive/violent acts is evident in terms of the frequency of such behavior. Parenting interventions (e.g. teaching parenting skills or building parents' capacities to manage children) reduces anti-social behavior. Community based interventions that engage violent perpetrators; particularly young men involved in gang-related activities, can also be effective. In Chicago for example where levels of violence are high, the NGO Ceasefire has succeeded in reducing shootings by up to 73%, and retaliatory shooting[s] by 100% in neighborhoods where it operates (www.ceasefirechicago.org). The programme is based on five core components: community mobilization, outreach to youth, the involvement of faith leaders, public education and strengthening community relations with the criminal justice system. Similar programs exist in violence-ridden communities in Brazil, Jamaica and other countries, suggesting that solutions do exist, but they lack the resources to scale up significantly.

Second, studies in Colombia and Guatemala (Moser 1997, Winton 2005), and interviews with women combatants in Sri Lanka and Nepal[iii] offer additional insight into the links between domestic and communal violence. In many instances, young women who joined gang or insurgencies stated that exposure to violence at home compelled them to flee and join the group. Gang membership provided protection, identity and emotional support to victims of abuse. Those joining insurgencies offer a mix of motivations. For some joining the fight was a means of escaping an abusive home or avenging their own victimization by state authorities; for others it was exacting revenge for the death of a loved one (father, husband, brother). Similarly, reconstructed narratives of the lives of female suicide bombers and interviews with some who failed in Palestine reveal a complex mix of political beliefs, religious ideology, [and] idealism mixed with emotional and social factors pertaining to their marital status or family life, that were manipulated by recruiters (often close relatives) that propelled women towards violence (Victor 2003).

Third, in addition to learning behavior in the domestic settings, young men and women are often recruited into state and non-state armed groups or gangs via social and familial networks. Among young men traveling to Iraq and Afghanistan to fight the 'jihad', friendship networks are key means of prompting recruitment and radicalization. The networks provide a sense of belonging, identity, and purpose. Fighting for the cause is a means of demonstrating courage or not losing face among cohorts. At the individual or relational levels, perpetrating violence – justified through ideology – is also a demonstration of masculinity (New York Times, Atran).

I.2 GENDER AND SEXUAL VIOLENCE DURING CONFLICT

In sum: The continuum of violence begins in the domestic and social setting and extends into the public sphere. High levels of social and gender based violence and inequality are indictors of fragility.

Sexual and other forms of gender-based violence (SGBV), defined by the World Health Organization (WHO) as "sexual and other forms of gender-based violence" comprises not only rape and attempted rape, but also sexual abuse, sexual exploitation, forced early marriage, domestic violence, marital rape, trafficking and female genital mutilation." SGBV has been a feature of warfare throughout time. For much of history it was neither recorded nor commented upon effectively. Even the Nuremberg trials took no significant notice of such crimes. It took Korean women victims of the Japanese army's forced prostitution activities over fifty years to gain acknowledgement of their plight.[iv]

SGBV remains an integral dimension of the contemporary trends in conflict and violence. But the extent and patterns of such violence are not similar across all settings. Although in cases such as the DRC [Editor's note: The Democratic Republic of the Congo] there is clear evidence of the exponential rise of such violence, in other cases it could be that greater awareness of the issues has prompted more attention and reporting.

Women and girls represent the overwhelming number of known victims of SGBV in most settings. Reports of male victimization are also emerging, but the taboo and silence enveloping male sexual violence and exploitation is still profound at all levels.[3]

In each context there are different drivers and motivations for the emergence and escalation of such violence. It is rarely conducted in a vacuum, and typically is the result of a mix of socio-cultural, political, [and] economic factors.

First, since the majority of violence experienced today takes place in civilian settings, civilians – including women – are directly targeted and impacted particularly by various forms of sexual and gender based violence. While in some settings (as discussed below) sexual violence is used as a deliberate tactic of war to sow fear in communities, prompt an exodus or to exude power and control, in many settings it is also a crime of opportunity and an extension of other forms of violence and insecurity.

"In a patriarchal society, domestic violence is actually recognized as one way of disciplining one's wife. In fact, even the society socializes you as a woman to anticipate this discipline. It is so deeply inculcated in many peoples' minds. We have women who say, when they have not been beaten, their husbands have stopped loving them."
Ann Njogu, Center for Rights Education and Awareness (CREAW), Kenya, March 2010
In Majtenyi, K. "Cases of Domestic Violence Increase in Kenya," www.voanews.com

It can also be a by-product of broader socio-cultural norms that perpetuate the notion that women are subordinate to men and can be treated as 'property'. A general culture of impunity for violence against women (VAW) can thus give rise to opportunistic violence during crises as in Guinea (2009), or post-tsunami Sri Lanka and Aceh in 2004[v] (Carballo et al 2006).

Second, sexual violence can be used as a war tactic. The threat and execution of rape can be a means of promoting displacement and ethnic cleansing as in Bosnia and Darfur. It can be used to assert control and suppress dissent. Used against men – as is now becoming more evident in the African Great Lakes region and other settings (e.g. Jamaica), it is a means of humiliation and emasculation. Women and men who are raped may be forced into silence for fear of being rejected by their families. In countries where sodomy and homosexuality is illegal, male rape victims in particular face double victimization (Refugee Law Project 2009); if they seek treatment they risk being reported to the police and criminalized. Their silence perpetuates impunity and heightens the chance of future attacks as well as health risks.

Third, sexual violence can be a strategic component of warfare or group violence. In internal conflicts and communal violence that pitch different communities against each other – be it on the basis of ethnicity, religion or gang affiliation – often the degradation and destruction of social fabric is a key strategic goal of fighting parties. During Rwanda's 100-day genocide, an estimated 300,000-400,000 women were raped[vi] (Rwandan Ministry of Social Affairs). Existing data indicates that 20,000 children were born of rape. In such instances, sexual violence against women (and men) including forced prostitution and impregnation, or rapes conducted publicly are profoundly damaging and thus effective. Women's bodies become the de facto frontlines as in the Balkans, where 20,000-50,000 women were raped – equal to 1.2% of the pre-war population (WHO). Again, men are also affected. In the Bosnian context there were reports of men being forced to sexually torture on one another[vii] and on female relatives. It is a mix of psychological and physical torture with long-term consequences.

Fourth, sexual violence and the oppression of women can also be a key element of the political or religious ideology of armed actors or states. This is evident among some Taliban and insurgency groups in Afghanistan and Pakistan. It feeds off deeply patriarchal cultures that condone discrimination, and certain interpretations of religious texts. The groups that condone such oppression often justify or couch it in terms of upholding cultural purity or pushing back against western cultural influences that are considered immoral, especially with regard to the status of women. This is particularly the case in honor-based societies.

Fifth, the seeming anonymity of perpetrators and context of chaos that is often portrayed in reporting belies a more ordered reality and possibilities for mitigating and limiting sexual violence and exploitation. From Nepal to Liberia, DRC and Colombia, armed actors including state police and military personnel are often key perpetrators. In some instances women and girls are abducted and forced into sex slavery, while in other instances, early marriage to military men has been a means of staving off abject poverty. Sexual exploitation and abuse (SEA) – ie. the "actual or attempted abuse of a position of vulnerability, differential power, or trust, for sexual purposes, including, but not limited to, profiting monetarily, socially or politically from the sexual exploitation of another, and "the actual or threatened phys-ical intrusion of a sexual nature, whether by force or under unequal or coercive conditions." (UN Secretary-General's Bulletin on protection from sexual exploitation and abuse (PSEA) (ST/SGB/2003/13)) – is another form of SGBV. It is also a common feature of displacement (see Box 1 for exam-ples). In addition to security forces [and] local actors, male relatives to international humanitarian and peacekeeping personnel (see Box 2) have been implicated. While imposing discipline on non-state actors may be difficult, punishment of state security services and international personnel impli-cated in SGBV is also minimal.

The long-term impact of SGBV committed in conflict is rarely addressed. Although there is limited data to determine the impact, incidences of SGBV can damage reconciliation efforts, hamper rehabilitation especially of victims, and fuel retributive violence. In addition, rates of sexual disease including HIV/AIDS among rape victims are thought to be high, though little data exists across countries. In Rwanda HIV prevalence in rural areas rose from 1 percent prior to the genocide in 1994 to 11 percent in 1997 (UNAIDS, WHO). A survey of 1000 Rwandan geno-cide widows conducted in 2000 revealed that 67 percent of rape survivors were HIV positive[viii] (AVEGA, WHO).

Regardless of the rationale, SGBV is neither an attack against women nor is it a one-off event. It has profound inflammatory impact on existing tensions (in gang or identity based settings), triggering revenge or retaliatory violence. It also has long term implications for development and recovery processes, ranging from the health care costs to address HIV/AIDS, to caring for orphans and rebuilding the broken trust within communities.

Patterns of Sexual Violence in Contemporary Conflict and Violence

The Balkans: By 1993 the Zenica Center for the Registration of War and Genocide Crime had documented 40,000 cases of war-related rape (UNFPA 2006).

Rwanda: In a 1999 survey of Rwandan women, 39% reported being raped during [the] 1994 genocide; 72% knew their rapists (UNFPA 2006).

Kosovo: An estimated 23,200 to 45,600 Kosovar Albanian women were believed to have been raped between August 1998-99 at the height of the conflict with Serbia (UNFPA 2006).

Liberia: In a 2003 random survey of 388 Liberian women in refugee camps, 74% reported sexual abuse prior to displacement, and 54% during displacement (UNFPA 2006). In a 2008 survey,

(continued from previous page)

42.2% of former female and 33% of male combatants (inc[luding] those associated with armed groups) had experienced sexual violence during the conflict (Johnson et al 2008, JAMA).

Colombia: Among 410 IDPs [internally displaced persons] in Cartagena, Colombia in 2003, 8% experienced sexual violence prior to displacement, and 11% during displacement (UNFPA 2006).

D.R. Congo: According to UN sources, an average of 1,100 rapes are reported each month, with gang rape being common (Women's Refugee Commission, 2009). The American Bar Association runs a sexual violence clinic in Goma, where some 10% of cases per month are male victims. The numbers of male victims are never fully known as most men and boys are reluctant to come forward. Many of those who did report were instantly shunned by their villages, ridiculed and called 'bush wives' (Gentleman; New York Times 2009).

(continued from previous page)

Burma: In 2005 it was estimated that 40,000 Burmese women were trafficked into Thailand each year to work in factories, brothels and domestic settings (Ward 2005).

Iraq: Accurate statistics are hard to come by, but UN news reports estimates that between 2003-2006, nearly 3,500 Iraqi women went missing; many sold or traded for sex work. Though difficult to ascertain, researchers predict that 25 percent were likely to be trafficked abroad with no knowledge of their own fate (IRIN 2006).

Iran: In the 2009 post election violence, male and female rape at the hands of state security forces generated significant public outcry and demands for investigation into prison practices by a presidential candidate (UK Channel 4 2009, CNNI 2009, Human Rights Watch 2010).

Peacekeepers, Sexual Exploitation and Abuse (SEA)

In 2000, civil society activists demanded accountability for UN peacekeepers implicated in sexual abuse and have continuously called for an increase in women peacekeepers as part of the solution to SEA committed by men. In addition SCr 1325 calls for 'gender and HIV/AIDs' awareness training.

In 2003 for the first time, the UN issued rules prohibiting sex with minors and prostitutes. In 2004, following reports of systemic sexual abuse by UN peacekeepers in the D.R. Congo, the UN implemented a 'zero-tolerance' policy. One case involved a 14-year old girl who was given two eggs in exchange for sex.

Between 2007-2010 UN troop contributing countries have reported disciplining 75 peacekeepers for sexual misconduct and other offences.

(continued from previous page)

In 2009 sexually related allegations against UN peacekeepers rose from 12% to a total of 55. Some of the allegations involved minors.

In 2009 the UN claims that member states responded to 14 out of 82 requests regarding sexually related investigations and their outcomes.

In 2009, over 80 international organizations signed a petition to the UN Secretary General (SG) demanding that the UN's most senior personnel in peacekeeping missions (such as the Special Representative of Secretary Generals, (SRSG)) should be held responsible and asked to resign for cases of abuse by peacekeepers and other personnel in his mission. The SG did not offer a response to this suggestion.

In 2010 there are 85,000 UN troops for 115 countries, serving in 16 missions. Many of the allegations of abuse are against civilian personnel.

(continued from previous page)

There are only 60 UN officials available to probe cases. They have no authority to discipline soldiers.

Steve Stecklow, Joe Lauria, "UN Peacekeepers Dodge Discipline in Sex-abuse Charges," Wall Street Journal, March 24, 2010.

I.3 FROM COMMUNAL TO PRIVATE VIOLENCE: GENDER AND THE CONTINUUM OF VIOLENCE

The continuum of violence from the public to the private space and from communal to ad hoc and domestic violence is most evident in post conflict settings and situations of chronic violence. For example, in a 2009 survey following the Israeli bombardments and invasion of Gaza 37 percent of women cited domestic violence as the primary safety problem facing women and girls in their communities, while over 50 percent of men cited public and political violence as the main security concern for men and boys.[ix] In other words the Israeli bombings and subsequent loss of homes and livelihoods made women feel more vulnerable to domestic abuse from their partners or relatives (perhaps as the means of venting frustration or seeking a sense of power in the domestic sphere in contrast to the humiliation meted out against

Palestinians by the Israeli forces). Men, however, were not fearful of rising domestic abuse. Their primary concern was increased risks in the public sphere.

The gendered dimensions of violence are pronounced as women and men in at-risk communities are affected by [it] in different ways. Women are at greater risk of oppression and sexual violence and exploitation. In Iraq for example, since the US invasion, the rise in religious extremism has been matched with increasing violence against women. Accurate statistics are hard to come by, but one estimates that between 2003-2006, nearly 3,500 Iraqi women went missing; many sold or traded for sex work. Though difficult to prove, UN news reports estimate that 25 percent were likely to be trafficked abroad with no knowledge of their own fate.[x] In DRC there was a 17-fold increase in rapes carried out by civilians between 2004-08, but many of the civilians may be former combatants (Harvard Humanitarian Initiative, Oxfam 2010).

Men on the other hand are more prone to violent deaths resulting from rising criminality and fragmentation of perpetrator groups. Throughout Central America men make up at least 88 percent of homicide victims. This is so widely accepted that there is little discussion. Concerns arise primarily in terms of the nature of death and increasing rates of murder.

Rise of Femicide in Guatemala

Femicide is defined as the murder of women because of their gender. In Guatemala there is impunity for 99% of femicide cases. The murder rate of women has increased by over 300% in the past decade.
• 2000 – 213 women killed
• 2003 – 383 [women killed]
• 2006 – 603 [women killed]
• 2009 – 708 [women killed]
Source: Guatemala Human Rights Commission/USA

But the gaps in gendered experiences of violence are also lessening. In Central America, targeted violence against women now includes femicide – deliberate murder of women – often coupled with sexual torture. The cause and motivation is not fully understood, but it is often assumed that such violence is tied to gangland reprisals. There is also a notable rise in reports of sexual violence against men. This too is part of a growing sensationalization of violence.

Various factors contribute to the rise of SGBV in post conflict and fragile settings.

1. *More Awareness/Better Reporting:* Increased awareness about gender based violence (GBV) and gender

disaggregated data collection has resulted in better understanding of the trends in violence and higher reporting. In war settings such as Liberia, the extent of SGBV was difficult to determine, but anecdotal evidence and post-war surveys prove extremely high rates particularly among women and men associated with armed actors. In post-conflict settings, SGBV has often shifted location to civilian settings. It is more evident and seemingly more prevalent.

2. *Higher Tolerance Threshold/Normalization of Violence*: Exposure to violence in the public sphere and during conflict and crises often results in the general normalization and higher tolerance thresholds for violence in the aftermath. Ex-combatants are often key perpetrators of SGBV, in part because it was condoned or ordered during conflict and was "normal" or accept-able behavior (UNDP, Blame it on the War, Forthcoming 2011).

3. *PTSD, Drug and Alcohol Abuse*: Higher levels of SGBV are also linked to the prevalence of posttraumatic stress disorder (PTSD) among returning combatants, witnesses and others exposed to the violence. PTSD and related alcohol or drug abuse are also factors in cases of suicide and homicide in the families and com-munities of ex-combatants. Recent documentation of such cases in the United States confirms the linkages.[xi]

4. *The availability of weapons*: In many post conflict and fragile states and communities, the easy availability and flow of small arms and light weapons (SALW) further exacerbates levels of violence. The

impact is evident not only in terms of emergent gang activities, criminality or police persecution, but also victimization of women in public and domestic settings (UNDP Idle Minds, Forthcoming 2011).

5. *Chronic Poverty and frustration* resulting from unemployment is also a contributing factor to levels of domestic violence, including child abuse and abandonment. Sexual exploitation of young girls is particularly rampant in many fragile settings – with predators ranging from relatives to teachers, pastors, bus drivers and other older men. Sexual abuse of boys is also prevalent in many settings, including countries with strict separation of the sexes. In Afghanistan for example, some poor families sell their pre-pubescent [boys] to older, richer men for "bacha bazi" (child/boy play).[xii] Where displacement, environmental damage or economic changes has resulted in the loss of traditional livelihoods, men's propensity for violence rises. It is linked to the inability to fulfill expected social roles that define manhood – having social prestige, being providers and protectors – triggering anger and depression. As the socially sanctioned "head of house or family", the domestic setting becomes the only domain in which they can assert their concept of masculinity, which often entails dominance. This can lead to physical and psychological abuse of wives, partners and offsprings.

6. *Often cramped living quarters* exacerbate conditions, making women and children more vulnerable to assault and sexual abuse from relatives and known perpetrators. Levels of reporting vary and are dependent

on the extent to which the police are trusted, fear of retribution and whether perpetrators are primary providers for the family.

I.4 EXISTING APPROACHES TO TACKLING THE PROBLEM OF SEXUAL GENDER BASED VIOLENCE (SGBV)

With many in the international women's rights and peace civil society-based movements pressing states and the international community, there has been a growing willingness to acknowledge the prevalence of SGBV in development and conflict settings. There is also growing understanding of SGBV as a weapon and tactic of conflict that threatens communal security. While there is still significant inertia and resistance to implementing strategies for the prevention and mitigation of such violence, there is some progress and innovation at the policy and programmatic levels.

I.4.i Policy & Normative Level Frameworks:

Internationally, since the mid-1990s with precedent set at the International Criminal Tribunals for Rwanda (ICTR) and Yugoslavia (ICTY) and the inclusion of SGBV into the Rome Statute of the International Criminal Court (ICC), significant progress has been made in terms of defining such crimes as war crimes and crimes against humanity. In 2008, in resolution 1820, the UN Security Council formally recognized sexual violence as a threat to peace and security.

The unanimous passage of security council resolutions (SCr) 1820 (2008) and 1888 (2009) following SCr 1325 (2000) have given attention and momentum to the issue of sexual violence. The resolutions have multiple state sponsors, thus providing stronger national ownership. They mandate the collection of data and systemic reporting of SGBV in countries on the Council's agenda. In 2010 the UN appointed the Special Representative for Sexual Violence, who will sustain attention to the issues globally.

The impact of such measures is notable in the case of Guinea. During protests against the military regime in Guinea in [the] September 2009 coup, reports of sexual violence by armed actors including military personnel were rife. Cell-phone images and YouTube video clips had profound impact. By 2010, the UN had instigated an inquiry and published a report that noted widespread and systemic attack by the Presidential Guard. The UN also took an unprecedented step of naming the head of state and a number of his associates as being potentially liable for crimes against humanity against civilians and the rape and sexual assault of at least 109 women. The international pressure and isolation prompted the leader of the military junta to scapegoat his senior colleagues and flee the country. A clear split in the military leadership opened space for mediation and steps towards civilian rule.

Perpetrators of sexual violence have not been brought to justice, but *"For those who fight for sexual violence to be taken seriously as a matter of collective peace and security, the international response to Guinea suggests progress. More importantly, for those who would wield rape as an instrument of war and terror, an ostensibly cheap and easy tactic of choice, it suggests heightened stakes and potential for political backfire."* (Anderson, Unifem/Democracy Now 2010).[xiii]

Nationally, a number of countries have initiated measures to address SGBV. Liberia has stringent legislation regarding rape cases, with perpetrators facing up to ten years in prison sentences. It also has a special court (Court E) dedicated to prosecuting cases of sexual violence.

Sierra Leone, Croatia and Afghanistan are among a growing number of countries with dedicated family units in police stations designed to enable reporting of domestic violence. The goal in most instances is to have trained officers – men and women – to handle cases sensitively. In Afghanistan efforts were made to provide safe housing for police trainees and to ensure that women officers were not seen as "unaccompanied."

The impact of such interventions is still unclear. In reality the units are too few and under resourced. The numbers of women police officers are still too few to affect change. More emphasis is needed to ensure that male officers are recognized for their efforts in protecting women, are provided the necessary training and capacity building and held accountable. Moreover there is a profound lack of quality human rights and protection training to police recruits in many countries. Community based policing interventions supported by UNDP are an important contribution. Similarly the training and tools developed by the Geneva Center for the Democratic Control of Armed Forces (DCAF) are significant resources. But neither gender sensitive policing nor the promotion of policing as a service to communities (rather than a force) is yet widespread.

I.4.ii Advocacy and Awareness Raising

There are a wide range of international and national level initiatives involving the UN in partnership with NGOs that are dedicated to raising awareness and action against SGBV. Civil society is often at forefront of demand for changes in state policies and laws. For example in Iran, the Million Signature Campaign to End Gender Discriminatory Laws, launched in 2006, has gained global attention, but received little support from multilateral organizations. In part this is due to the isolation that Iranian civil society is facing as a result of the Iranian government's status internationally. There is limited access and connection between Iranian civil society and their counterparts elsewhere. It is also due to the fact that the campaign is indigenous and independent and not funded by international actors. This can lead to less attention and less understanding of their goal and actions. Similarly as noted above, Afghan women's demands for protection and justice gain little or no concrete support from countries directly engaged in the conflict. In this case attention to the state and security threats that are prioritized by the international community override the concerns voiced by Afghan women.

Liberia has been the exception to the rule. While it is difficult to ascertain all the factors contributing to its success in addressing SGBV, four stand out. First, reports of the intensity and extent of SGBV in Liberia during the war were widely disseminated. Second, women played a pivotal role in securing a peace process, removing Charles Taylor from office and mobilizing public support for Ellen Johnson

Sirleaf. Third, President Sirleaf publicly acknowledged the contributions of women to peace and vowed to address their security needs. She was fully aware of the nature and impact of sexual violence in conflict, particularly since 2000 when she was selected as one of two experts to travel conflict zones globally and co-author UNIFEM's 2002 study on "Women, War and Peace." Fourth, President Sirleaf's willingness to address SGBV issues in Liberia was met by significant donor support. The governments of Denmark, Sweden and the US are among those supporting women's empowerment, and SGBV prevention and protection. In effect a mix of national leadership, strong civil society and international support has enabled the Liberian state to pay attention and seek solutions to the challenges of SGBV.

NGOs both national and international are at the forefront of awareness raising initiatives in many fragile settings. The Men Engage network and organizations such as Men's Resources International are leading efforts to raise issues of SGBV with men in communities. The results from such initiatives are promising. But they operate on small scales and can be time/process intensive [so] that up scaling remains a challenge.

I.4.iii Tackling SGBV: Some Progress but Not Enough
At the international level, the discourse and practice regarding SGBV overwhelmingly pertains to "response" rather than prevention. In effect responsibility for SGBV is relegated to justice and rule of law programmes, with a strong focus on "reporting" of cases, police responses, the provision of shelters and care for victims. While such response mechanisms are essential, and can contribute to lessening impunity, they are not sufficient.

The 5 Pillars of the DRC Comprehensive Strategy on Combating Sexual Violence

- 1. Protection and prevention (UNHCR)
- 2. Ending impunity for perpetrators (Joint Human Rights Office - MONUC/OHCHR)
- 3. Security sector reform (MONUC SSR)
- 4. Assistance for victims of sexual violence (UNICEF)
- 5. Data and mapping (UNFPA)

The situation is evolving however. In DRC for example in 2009, the UN system launched the "Comprehensive Strategy on Combating Sexual Violence." Endorsed by the government and involving collaboration with a mix of state, NGO and UN entities, it is a major attempt at coordinating and tackling SGBV from multiple angles. The strategy comprises 5 pillars (see box) and an operational plan for national and provincial level action has been developed with a budget of $56 million over 2 years.

More systemic and strategic effort is still needed to mitigate SGBV incidences in urban slums, displacement camps or rural areas. But given that governments (even those that are committed to the issues) lack the means to provide direct services to communities and victims, it is imperative to ensure criteria that allow for an efficient and channeling funds to service providers. In most instances NGOs and CBOs are at the frontlines of providing service to victims and instigating awareness raising and violence prevention efforts. Yet many providers have no access and no means of holding their governments accountable.

While there is increasing attention to the prevalence of PTSD and other forms of mental illness including depression among war and violence-affected communities – all of which can be contributing factors to higher rates of SGBV – responses or interventions to tackle this issue are negligible in most settings. Framed as a 'health' issue, resources are rarely available for diagnosing or treating mental illness within the framework of post-conflict recovery, when much of the funds and focus of international actors is on security, state institution building and macro-economic recovery. Disarmament Demobilization and Reintegration (DDR) programmes could provide an important entry point for addressing the issues. This could also be an opportunity to raise awareness of sexual violence among ex-fighters. But most DDR programmes do not have this approach. Attention to these 'soft issues' – which are often the hardest and most complex to tackle, is missing. This gap has profound implications for post conflict crime and ultimately prevention of new cycles of violence.

Similarly, although funding for SGBV has increased, there is often uneven distribution across the key sectors. Health and judicial services may be funded but security sector reform may not be tackled as aggressively. Service provision can be hampered by lack of transportation and capacity at the national level – particularly in terms of psychosocial care. Additionally the emphasis on judicial and legal justice inadvertently marginalizes victims' basic needs. For them recovery, protection and future prevention is often tied to their ability to move on and generate incomes for themselves and children. (Mantilla/World Bank 2006, IRIN 2009)[xiv]

There are innovative efforts underway and a number of practical recommendations that if implemented could contribute to the challenge.

- UNHabitat's "Safe Cities" programme addresses SGBV prevention issues through the lens of urban space planning. Consultations with women in areas of high violence help identify key locations and times of attack, and together solutions are sought. They can range from the provision of street lighting (also beneficial to other community members) to design of housing or redevelopment of wasted space for recreational activities to limit opportunities for crime and sexual assault in public settings.

- The Women's Commission for Refugee Women and Children (WCRWC) has been at the forefront of research on SGBV issues in displacement settings. They offer a number of practical recommendations for mitigating such violence. For example women are often at high risk of attack when collecting firewood for cooking. WCRWC has long advocated the regular and systematic provision of cooking fuel or non-cooking food to women in displaced settings to limit their exposure to risk. In Darfur WCRWC advocated for the provision of 'firewood patrols' to accompany and protect women. Inclusion of women in the design and establishment of camps or urban settings is also crucial, as they can point to practical measures (e.g. placement of latrines,

washing facilities or other services they use regularly)
to limit their exposure to risk.

- In Nicaragua, local CBOs in partnership with
international NGO PATH, have developed social media
messaging including radio soap operas to promote
respectful treatment of women and girls. The 'entre
amigas' initiative (between girlfriends) also promotes
peer-based education to convey information regarding safe sexual practices, HIV/AIDS and violence. The
programme also includes a girls' soccer team that helps
promote self-confidence, trust and a support network
among adolescent girls in at-risk communities. Outreach
to boys is also included with a focus on promoting gender
equity and challenging machismo and aggressive male
gender norms. The peer-to-peer approach of the initiative is an effective means of reaching adolescents and
young people that are often most at risk yet [the] hardest
to engage in standard governmental initiatives.

- Identification and targeting of perpetrators of SGBV is
also essential. Too often the discourse is 'women are
raped' with no indication of the key actors. It seems cha-
otic and unknown but often the perpetrators and those
who condone the actions are known. A key approach
must be to target perpetrator groups to end all forms
of SGBV. In Afghanistan for example, through its Men's
Leadership Program, Women for Women International
trained 400 mullahs to incorporate the value of protecting
women's rights and its value to the society and economy
into their Friday prayers. While in the DRC, a leader of
an armed unit that practiced rape habitually banned the
practice on learning about the spread of HIV/AIDS.[xv]

- The attention to community driven development (CDD) and similar approaches is another important strategy for addressing gender dimensions of violence and recovery, especially given women's increased socio-economic activities at the community level. But international actors need to ensure effective representation of women in their interactions with local stakeholders. Sometimes the rush to embrace local or traditional actors and institutions as a means of building a community base can be detrimental for women and youth as often existing structures are dominated by local oligarchy with little interests in promoting women's empowerment or opening space for youth and other marginalized sectors of the community. They view the 'gender' question as a direct threat to socio-cultural identity and the imposition of western norms and morals. Identification of key champions and conduits into the community are therefore important steps. Similarly direct engagement and empowerment of women at the community level to participate in security discourse and advocacy can be a key means of promoting accountability from the ground up. In Sri Lanka, the Mothers and Daughters of Lanka (MDL) and in Nepal, the Women's Security Network (WSN) are examples of national NGOs, engaging and offering state security actors training in protection and prevention of SGBV. They also empower women to hold state security actors accountable. A multi-country Women's Security Campaign is also being proposed by the International Civil society Action Network (ICAN) and the MIT Center for International Studies in partnership with local NGOs.

1.5 CONCLUDING REFLECTIONS

In conflict or non-conflict settings, SGBV is a pervasive form of insecurity, affecting women, men, boys and girls, and implicating state and non-state actors.

These issues pose a significant challenge for multilateral organizations that are caught between opposing forces and interests. On the one hand, universal human rights standards coupled with the demands of women in communities (victims and human rights defenders who put themselves at risk to uphold universal values) mandates attention to the security and protection needs of women. There is an understanding that women's protection also results in better protection for children and the community at large.

On the other hand, multilateral entities dominated by state interests must prioritize building state capacities in contexts where governance systems are weak. Yet often-times their key national counterparts are actors implicated in corruption or fomenting violence. In effect, by supporting them, international entities further legitimize and empower such actors. This also poses a challenge as the solutions that are developed may lack legitimacy in the eyes of the public. As the 2011 events in the Middle East indicate the tendency towards achieving 'stability' through support for illegitimate leaders can ultimately reach a breaking point.

One means of resolving this is by ensuring the inclusion of civil society voices in transition and peace negotiations processes. As the findings of a 2008 study suggest "durable agreements...feature direct civil society participation in peace negotiations, particularly in conflicts characterized by undemocratic elites....[I]n negotiations among democratic elites, civil society can participate effectively by influencing their respective political representatives and these agreements seem to be as durable as those featuring high civil society participation alone. This suggests a hierarchy of preferential partners for mediation: the ideal parties for durable peace agreements are democratic elites without civil society groups at the table, but with regular civil society influence on those elites. If elites are not democratic representatives, then direct civil society involvement in peace negotiations may increase the durability of agreements reached" (Wanis-St.John, Kew, JIN 2008).

Moreover, international development agencies are not attuned or equipped to addressing the socio-cultural factors that contribute to gender based inequality and tolerance of GBV. Yet to tackle such violence, a local socio-cultural framing is essential. Instead of assuming that sexual violence is a tolerated or socially accepted mode of behavior, it is essential to highlight it as a profoundly unacceptable practice that is symptomatic of a breakdown of socio-cultural norms and taboos. Preventive and protective strategies therefore must also draw on cultural, religious, [and] historic precedence, [and] directives and laws that promote protection and respect for women. One approach can be to recruit respected male leaders to denounce sexual violence and frame masculinity and manhood as the ability and willingness to protect women against such harm rather than to perpetrate it. Another approach is to condemn the acts publicly. Raising awareness and public demand for accountability are important strategies for challenging the status quo. Outreach and collaboration with community elders and faith leaders can also yield positive results. If they condemn the acts other men may heed their words and societal tolerance can diminish. Practical steps such as providing victims access to justice and long term care are important and can convince victims to report cases. In Pakistan NGOs such as Bedari use street theatre to bring the issues to public attention and generate understanding and awareness.

In addition, the pervasive and profound impact of PTSD and violence-related trauma cannot be ignored or minimized. There is direct correlation between such trauma and violence, thus tackling it must be a priority component of recovery programmes. The scale of the problem is beyond the capacity of many health systems, let alone those of fragile states. International institutions are either not equipped or mandated to address this need.

The process or 'how' things are done becomes as important as the actual goal or 'what is done.' For example, international actors must also acknowledge that in fragile settings, particularly where poverty and unemployment among men is also high, a heavy push for women's empowerment without attention to backlash and reactions of men can prompt a rise in SGBV against women. This does not suggest abandoning a rights-based agenda for women. Rather it calls for programming that draws men into the process, and demonstrates that value of equality and economic empowerment for women and men. Emerging men-engage initiatives are a step in the right direction. But for large-scale impact, the awareness and capacities of national government personnel to assess the gender dimensions of economic and social recovery must be enhanced.

Finally, there is a question of how far and fast should such issues be raised. Here too, women can guide and navigate the discussions. There is no homogeneity across or within countries. Rural and urban women have different priorities and concerns. They also have different levels and means of influence privately and publicly. They are best placed to identify the reactions and needs of their male counterparts. In addition, drawing men into the discourse about women's security and participation is critical. While patriarchal norms prevail in many societies, crises and transitions also expose men to the challenges that women face and their resilience. It can shift attitudes and create openings for more equitable engagement. From a programmatic standpoint this means ensuring that assessments include questions and exploration of men and women's needs and attitudes. One simple step can be to ask men about issues that are traditionally 'women's issues,' while engaging women in discussions and analysis of issues that are typically considered outside their domain, yet about which they often have opinions and knowledge. In Pakistan for example, women peace and development practitioners are involved in the deradicalization of youth away from Taliban and extremist forces.

Tackling SGBV requires coordinated approaches that address the social, political, [and] economic empowerment of potential and actual victims, while addressing security needs, and embracing preventive, protective and punitive measures. It requires full part-nership and cooperation between state and non-state actors, national and community level stakeholders. Facilitating such partnerships is a minimum but crucial contribution that multilateral actors can make.

1. What are some of the long-term impacts of experiencing or witnessing domestic violence?

2. Choose two countries listed in this article. Compare and contrast the findings about them.

"FEMALE VICTIMS OF SEXUAL VIOLENCE, 1994-2010" BY MICHAEL PLANTY, LYNN LANGTON, ET AL., FROM THE US DEPARTMENT OF JUSTICE, MAY 31, 2016

[Editor's note: Figures and tables for this article are not included here and can be found with the original paper.]

From 1995 to 2005, the total rate of sexual violence committed against U.S. female residents age 12 or older declined 64% from a peak of 5.0 per 1,000 females in 1995 to 1.8 per 1,000 females in 2005 (figure 1, appendix table 1). It then remained unchanged from 2005 to 2010. Sexual violence against females includes completed, attempted, or threatened rape or sexual assault. In 2010, females nationwide experienced about 270,000 rape or sexual assault victimizations, compared to about 556,000 in 1995.

Completed rape or sexual assault accounted for more than 50% of the total rape or sexual violent victimizations in 2010. Between 1995 and 2010, the rate of completed rape or sexual assault declined from 3.6 per 1,000 females to 1.1 per 1,000. Over the same period, the rates of attempted rape or sexual assault and victimizations involving the threat of rape remained relatively stable.

HIGHLIGHTS

From 1995 to 2010, the estimated annual rate of female rape or sexual assault victimizations declined [64%], from 5.0 victimizations per 1,000 females age 12 or older to [1.8] per 1,000.

In 2005-10, females who were age 34 or younger, who lived in lower income households, and who lived in rural areas experienced some of the highest rates of sexual violence.

In 2005-10, 78% of sexual violence involved an offender who was a family member, intimate partner, friend, or acquaintance.

In 2005-10, the offender was armed with a gun, knife, or other weapon in 11% of rape or sexual assault victimizations.

The percentage of rape or sexual assault victimizations reported to police increased to a high of 59% in 2003 before declining to 32% in 2009 and 2010.

The percentage of females who were injured during a rape or sexual assault and received some type of treatment for their injuries increased from 26% in 1994-98 to 35% in 2005-10.

In 2005-10, about 80% of female rape or sexual assault victims treated for injuries received care in a hospital, doctor's office, or emergency room, compared to 65% in 1994-98.

In 2005-10, about 1 in 4 (23%) rape or sexual assault victims received help or advice from a victim service agency.

The data in this report were drawn from the Bureau of Justice Statistics' (BJS) National Crime Victimization Survey (NCVS). The NCVS collects information on nonfatal crimes reported and not reported to the police from a nationally representative sample of persons age 12 or older who live in U.S. households. Persons are interviewed every 6 months over 3 years with the first interview conducted in person and follow-up interviews conducted either in person or by phone.

The NCVS produces national rates and levels of violent and property victimization, as well as information on the characteristics of crimes and victims and the consequences of victimization. Because the NCVS collects information from victims, it does not measure homicide.

Unless noted, this report presents estimates for the aggregate of rape or sexual assault victimizations. The term sexual violence is used throughout to refer to rape or sexual assault victimizations, including attempts and threats. Victimization is the basic unit of analysis used throughout the report, and the number of victimizations is equal to the number of victims present during a criminal incident.

Trend estimates are based on 2-year rolling averages centered on the most recent year. For example, estimates reported for 2010 represent the average estimates for 2009 and 2010. For other tables in this report, the focus is on aggregate data from 1994 through 1998, 1999 through 2004, and 2005 through 2010. These methods of analysis improve the reliability and stability of comparisons over time and between subgroups. For additional estimates not included in this report, see the NCVS Victimization Analysis Tool (NVAT) on the BJS website.

Measuring sexual violence using the NCVS

This report focuses on sexual violence that includes completed, attempted, and threatened rape or sexual assault. NCVS survey respondents are asked to respond to a series of questions about the nature and characteristics of their victimization. The NCVS classifies victimizations as rape or sexual assault even if other crimes, such as robbery or assault occur at the same time. The NCVS then uses the following rape and sexual assault definitions:

Rape is the unlawful penetration of a person against the will of the victim, with use or threatened use of force, or attempting such an act. Rape includes psychological coercion and physical force, and forced sexual intercourse means vaginal, anal, or oral penetration by the offender. Rape also includes incidents where penetration is from a foreign object (e.g., a bottle), victimizations against male and female victims, and both heterosexual and homosexual rape. Attempted rape includes verbal threats of rape.

Sexual assault is defined across a wide range of victimizations, separate from rape or attempted rape. These crimes include attacks or attempted attacks generally involving unwanted sexual contact between a victim and offender. Sexual assault may or may not involve force and includes grabbing or fondling. Sexual assault also includes verbal threats.

The measurement of rape and sexual assault presents many challenges. Victims may not be willing to reveal or share their experiences with an interviewer. The level and type of sexual violence reported by victims is sensitive to how items are worded, definitions used, data collection mode, and a variety of other factors related to the interview process. In addition, the legal definitions of rape and sexual assault vary across jurisdictions. The NCVS presents one approach to measuring and enumerating these incidents as well as other forms of violence and property crime. (For more information about the technical aspects of the NCVS, see *Methodology*.)

IN 2005-10, FEMALES WHO WERE AGE 34 OR YOUNGER, WHO LIVED IN LOWER INCOME HOUSEHOLDS, AND WHO LIVED IN RURAL AREAS HAD SOME OF THE HIGHEST RATES OF SEXUAL VIOLENCE

The rate of sexual violence against females declined with age. In 2005-10, sexual violence was committed against females ages 12 to 34 at a rate of about 4 victimizations per 1,000, compared to a rate of 1.5 victimizations per 1,000 for females ages 35 to 64 and 0.2 per 1,000 for age 65 or older (table 1). This pattern was consistent across all three aggregate time periods. Over time, the rate of sexual violence declined for both the 12-to-17 and 18-to-24 age groups. Females ages 12 to 17 had the largest decline, from 11.3 per 1,000 in 1994-98 to 4.1 in 2005-10.

For all racial and ethnic groups, the rate of sexual violence was lower in 2005-10 than it was in 1994-98. Within each time period, few differences existed in the rates of sexual violence across racial and ethnic groups. Non-Hispanic white females and black and Hispanic females had a similar rate of sexual violence over time. However, Hispanic females had lower rates of sexual violence than black females in 1999-04 and in 2005-10. Although American Indians and Alaska Natives appeared to experience rape or sexual assault victimization at rates higher than other racial and ethnic groups, these rates were based on small sample sizes and are not reliable.

Across all three time periods between 1994 and 2010, females who had never been married or who were divorced or separated at the time of the interview had higher rates of rape or sexual assault victimization than females who were married or widowed.[1] From 1994 to 2010, females who had never been married, those who were divorced or separated, and those who were married experienced about a 50% decline in the rate of sexual violence.

Consistently across all three time periods, females living in households in the lowest income bracket (less than $25,000 annually) experienced rape or sexual assault victimization at higher rates than females in higher income brackets. In 2005-10, females in households earning less than $25,000 per year experienced 3.5 rape or sexual assault victimizations per 1,000 females, compared to 1.9 per 1,000 in households earning between $25,000 and $49,999 and 1.8 per 1,000 in households earning $50,000 or more.

In 1994-98, the rate of rape or sexual assault victimization for females living in urban areas (5.1 per 1,000) was higher than the rate for females in suburban (3.9 per 1,000) and rural

(3.9 per 1,000) areas. In 2005-10 this pattern reversed, and the rate of sexual violence for females in rural areas (3.0 per 1,000) was higher than the rate of sexual violence for females in urban (2.2 per 1,000) and suburban (1.8 per 1,000) areas.

THE PERCENTAGE OF RAPE OR SEXUAL ASSAULT VICTIMIZATIONS THAT OCCURRED AT OR NEAR THE VICTIM'S HOME INCREASED OVER TIME

In 2005-10, about 55% of rape or sexual assault victimizations occurred at or near the victim's home, and another 12% occurred at or near the home of a friend, relative, or acquaintance (table 2). The percentage of sexual violence that occurred at or near the home of the victim increased from 49% in 1994-98 to 55% in 2005-10. In comparison, the percentage of sexual violence that occurred at or near the home of a friend or in a commercial place or parking lot declined between 1994-98 and 2005-10. The number of rape or sexual assault victimizations occurring at or near the victim's home declined at a slower rate over time compared to the number of victimizations that occurred outside the home (not shown in table).

Over all three periods, between 41% and 48% of victims of sexual violence were undertaking activities at or around their homes at the time of the incident. In 2005-10, 12% of rape or sexual assault victimizations against females occurred while the victim was working, and 7% occurred while the victim was attending school. Another 29% of sexual violence occurred while the victim went to or from work or school, was out shopping, or was engaged in leisure activities away from the home.

ABOUT 3 IN 4 VICTIMS OF SEXUAL VIOLENCE KNEW THE OFFENDER

About 90% of rape or sexual assault victimizations involved one offender, a percentage that was stable across the three periods (table 3). In 2005-10, most rape or sexual assault victims (78%) knew the offender. About 34% of all rape or sexual assault victimizations were committed by an intimate partner (former or current spouse, girlfriend, or boyfriend), 6% by a relative or family member, and 38% by a friend or acquaintance. Strangers committed about 22% of sexual violence, a percentage that was also unchanged from 1994 to 2010.

In 2005-10, about half of rape or sexual assault victimizations were committed by an offender age 30 or older (table 4). Fifteen percent of offenders were age 17 or younger and 34% were ages 18 to 29. These percentages were stable across the three periods from 1994 to 2010.

Across all three periods, white males committed the majority of sexual violence.[2] Over time, the percentage of sexual violence committed by white offenders declined from 70% in 1994-98 to 57% in 2005-10. The percentage of black offenders increased from 18% in 1994-98 to 27% in 2005-10. White males consistently accounted for more than 82% of the total U.S. male population and black males accounted for 11%. The NCVS did not collect information on the ethnicity of the offender. Therefore, Hispanic offenders make up an unknown portion of the white, black, and other race of offender categories.

Consistent across all three periods, about 40% of victims believed the offender had been drinking or using drugs prior to the victimization. In 2005-10, in 30% of the victimizations the victim did not believe the offender had been drinking or using drugs, and in 30% the victim did not know whether there had been substance use.

ABOUT 1 IN 10 RAPE OR SEXUAL ASSAULT VICTIMIZATIONS INVOLVED A WEAPON

Across all three periods, the offender in the majority of rape or sexual assault victimizations did not have a weapon (table 5). In 2005-10, victims reported that the offender possessed or used a weapon in 11% of all sexual violence. The victim reported that the offender had a firearm in 6% of victimizations and a knife in 4%. The percentage of offenders armed with a weapon increased from 6% in 1994-98 to 11% in the two later periods. The NCVS does not ask victims if they were incapacitated in some manner, such as being drugged or intoxicated.

THE PERCENTAGE OF FEMALE VICTIMS OF SEXUAL VIOLENCE WHO RECEIVED MEDICAL TREATMENT INCREASED BETWEEN 1994-98 AND 2005-10

In 2005-10, 58% of female victims of sexual violence suffered a physical injury during the victimization, such as cuts, bruises, internal injuries, broken bones, gunshot wounds, or rape injuries (table 6). Of the females who suffered an injury in 2005-10, 35% said that they received some type of treatment for their injuries, an increase from 26% in 1994-98. About 80% of victims who received treatment for their injuries in 2005-10 received this care in a hospital, doctor's office, or emergency room. The other 20% were treated at the scene, in their home, at a neighbor or friend's house, or in some other location. In comparison, in 1994-98, 65% of treated victims received care in a hospital, doctor's office, or emergency room, while 35% received first aid or treatment at the scene, at home, at a neighbor or friend's house, or in some other location.

In 2005-10, about 1 in 4 victims of sexual violence received help or advice from a private or public victim service agency (table 7). This percentage remained stable over the three periods.

THE PERCENTAGE OF SEXUAL VIOLENCE REPORTED TO POLICE INCREASED TO A HIGH OF 59% IN 2003 BEFORE DROPPING TO 32% IN 2009 AND 2010

In 1995, 28% of rape or sexual assault victimizations against females were reported to police. This percentage increased to 59% in 2003 before declining to 32% in 2009 and 2010.

Of the 36% of rape or sexual assault victimizations reported to police in 2005-10, about 64% were reported directly by the victims, an increase from 50% in 1994-98 (table 8). The percentage of victimizations known to police because they were reported by another household member declined from 26% in 1994-98 to 10% in 2005-10, while the percentage reported by an official other than the police increased from 4% to 14%.

Of the rape or sexual assault victimizations that were reported to police in 2005-10, 28% were reported in an attempt to protect the victim from future victimizations, and 25% were reported to try to stop or prevent escalation of the victimization as it was occurring (table 9). Among rape or sexual assault victimizations that went unreported, the most common reason victims gave for not reporting the crime during 2005-10 was fear of reprisal (20%). The percentage of victimizations that went unreported because the victim considered the incident a personal matter declined from 23% in 1994-98 to 13% in 2005-10.

A LOWER PERCENTAGE OF SEXUAL VIOLENCE REPORTED TO POLICE RESULTED IN ARRESTS IN 2005-10 (31%) THAN IN 1994-98 (47%)

The police may take a variety of actions in response to reported rape or sexual assault victimizations. During 2005-10, about 84% of victims stated that police came to the victim after being called, up from 75% during 1994-98 (table 10). About 1 in 10 victims who reported went directly to the police to report the incident, a percentage that has remained stable over time (not shown in [table]).

Across all three periods, when police responded after being notified, the most common police activity was to take a report from the victim, followed by questioning witnesses or conducting a search for the offender (table 11). In 2005-10, police took the victim's report in 86% of victimizations reported to police, and the police questioned witnesses or conducted a search in 48% of cases. During the same period, about 19% of victims reported that the police collected evidence, up from 8% in 1994-98.

The percentage of reported rape or sexual assault victimizations against females that resulted in an arrest either at the scene or during a follow-up investigation decreased, from 47% in 1994-98 to 31% in 2005-10 (not shown in table). Out of the 283,200 annual average rape or sexual assault victimizations in 2005-10 both reported and not reported to the police, approximately 12% resulted in an arrest at the scene or during a follow-up investigation.

1. Choose one statistical change during the time periods outlined in this article. What are some of the reasons those changes could have taken place?

"THE MEDIA AND GENDER-BASED MURDERS OF WOMEN: NOTES ON THE CASES IN EUROPE AND LATIN AMERICA" BY CLAUDIA PAOLA LAGOS LIRA AND PATSILI TOLEDO, FROM HEINRICH BÖLL FOUNDATION, JULY 24, 2014

INTRODUCTION

Violence against women, especially its most severe form, femicide/feminicide, is caused by many factors, such as social constructs and the symbolic violence of what it means to be a man or a women in different societies. In contemporary societies, mass media plays a fundamental role in these constructs due both to the content, language and narrative used, and to audience consumption. This article analyses the connections between gender-based murders of women and the media coverage of these murders, particularly in Europe and Latin America. What effect, if any, does the broadcasting and coverage of murders of women have on the victims and perpetrators, and on society as a whole? What role can or should journalism and the media play in violence against women? Is regulation necessary and/or legitimate?

I. FEMALE HOMICIDE AND GENDER-BASED VIOLENCE

Homicide is a serious crime everywhere. It violates an individual's right to life and has terrible consequences for society as a whole, in the form of the suffering which the loss of a loved one causes and the feelings of public insecurity that homicide provokes, which in turn erode social and human capital and undermine community development (Ganpat et al, 2011: 10). The United Nations Office on Drugs and Crime (UNODC, 2011) confirmed that there has been a decrease in homicides at global level in the last few decades, but this decrease does not apply to female homicides. While they still represent a minority of total homicides, women are the main victims of domestic or intimate partner violence, crimes which are not decreasing over time. Nearly 40% of women murdered all over the world have died at the hands of their intimate partners (WHO, 2013). Despite the significance of the phenomenon, in many countries information on the relationship between the perpetrator and victim is not recorded, or is only partially recorded (WHO, 2013).

Female homicides have gained more social and media attention in recent decades. From the reporting of cases of disappearance, sexual violence and murders of women in Ciudad Juárez, Mexico, the use of the expression feminicide or femicide has been extended in Latin America to refer to gender-based homicides of women, including cases where women are killed by their partners or former partners. These cases, called intimate femicides, make up the majority of female homicides at global level, as indicated by the UNODC.

Europe too, has started to pay more attention to femicides, particularly those committed by partners or former partners, under a variety of official terms: feminicide/femicide, domestic violence, mortal victims of gender-based violence, and male violence against women, among others. Although in the majority of countries there are no regular statistics in this respect, in countries where they have been evaluated, e.g. in Germany, it has been found that half of the women murdered were killed by their partners or former partners. In France, the number of women murdered due to "domestic violence" increased by more than 20% between 2001 and 2012 and in Italy, the feminist organisations that record these deaths have reported a sustained increase in the murders of women in recent years. In Spain, there has been an official record of mortal victims of gender-based violence since 2003. These records confirm that intimate femicide is usually the corollary of previous violence by partners or former partners against women, i.e. they are not isolated violent incidents. This underlines the role that policies regarding gender-based violence in intimate relationships may have in preventing femicide and protecting women.

In Latin America, women's organisations from various countries started to record these cases over a decade ago, and in recent years limited official statistics have also been available. While the real situation in the continent is heterogeneous, several countries present alarming rates of femicide/feminicide. In general, the number of gender-based female homicides in Latin America where the perpetrators were the women's partners is the third highest worldwide, after Southeast Asia and Africa (WHO, 2013).

Regional differences can be explained by the differences in homicide patterns in general and according to the degree of cultural tolerance toward violence against women.

II. THE MEDIA AND VIOLENCE AGAINST WOMEN

As when talking about violence against women and the cultural contexts in which it takes place, when referring to the media, it should be noted that there are also major differences between the media systems in different countries and regions (Hallin and Mancini, 2012 and 2004; Waisbord, 2000). Certain cultural matrices are particularly important to consider and are central to the subject at hand.

Different television cultures can offer differing narratives and propose disparate visions of society. In this way, the narrativity of the news varies depending on the countries and their cultures: in some European countries, there is no room for the narrative techniques of fiction (music, close-ups, reiteration, melodrama), which are central to the narrative structure of the media in more sensationalist Latin America.

The role of the media in the production and reproduction of gender stereotypes, and particularly of gender-based violence, has been a source of concern in feminist studies for many decades (Mattelart, 2003).

This concern has given rise to research into the place of women, and especially violence against them, in areas such as media production processes, gender representations in the media and debates and content in general in the media, among others.

With regard to news production, we can note the low proportion of women working in editorial offices and in high-level editorial positions (IWMF, 2010). Furthermore, various studies demonstrate that hegemonic news values continue to correspond to a male-dominated culture which permeates journalistic routines in newsrooms (Tsui and Lee 2012; Zeldes, Fico and Diddi, 2012; Ross and Carter, 2011; Zeldes and Fico, 2010; Vega, 2010a and 2012, cited in CNTV, 2013).

Furthermore, different studies in various countries have noted an over-representation of violence and discrimination against women and girls in news content, especially news that is broadcast on television (Rovetto, 2013, on CNTV, 2013: 25).

POSSIBLE EFFECTS OF NEWS COVERAGE OF FEMICIDE/FEMINICIDE:

a) Presenting violence against women as an individual or relationship problem

Four frames have been identified in the media coverage of femicide/feminicide and violence against women: 1) a police frame or "just the facts"; 2) a frame indicating that these events happen to people who are different [than] "us"; 3) a frame that blames the victims and/or excuses the perpetrator; 4) a frame that implies shock at how "normal" the perpetrator identified appears (Gillespie et al, 2013).

Police frames or "just the facts" favour a sensationalist view, where gruesome details – such as the number of times [the] victim was stabbed – or other specific details of the attack are highlighted. This frame is frequent in Latin America but it also exists in Europe. The media often refers to jealousy or the use of drugs or alcohol, uncritically justifying the actions of the perpetrator of the crime, or including expressions like "from love to murder" or "crime of passion," portraying the homicides as "love stories."

These frames maintain a critical disconnection between femicides/feminicides, presented as isolated, individual cases, and domestic violence as a broader social problem (Gillespie et al, 2013). A recent study carried out in Sweden shows that the majority of news studied describes violence as the result of imbalances in the family system, placing the focus of the problem at [the] individual level, which prevents violence [from] being considered a social problem (Halili, 2013).

In Italy, feminist organisations recently reported the inappropriate treatment in the press of femicide/feminicide cases, for instance, that are described as family tragedies and not as violence against women, or that indicate depression due to the loss of a job as a justification, or that insist on interviewing neighbours only to show that the murderer was a good man.

In the United Kingdom, as a result of the Leveson investigation, various women's organisations presented information on news coverage of violence against women in 2012 described as either "intrusive, inaccurate, which misrepresented or which were misogynistic, victim-blaming or condoning of VAWG," giving several examples.

b) The copy-cat effect

A particularly significant aspect in the field of mass communication research is whether the media can affect individuals' behaviour. There is evidence that this has occurred in cases of youth suicide (Malmuth and Briere, 1986).

The copy-cat effect is mentioned in various reports in relation to cases of women burned with acid in countries like Bangladesh, India and Cambodia, where it is maintained that the increase in cases of women burned in this way may be due to the copy-cat effect (Kalantry and Kestenbaum, 2011: 10).

The case of Cambodia is of special interest: on 5 December 1999, singer Tat Marina was attacked with acid and the case was highly publicised. Before this case, the number of acid attacks recorded was relatively low, but since then there has been a sharp increase in these types of attacks (Kalantry and Kestenbaum, 2011). Between

December 1999 and May 2000, there were 15 attacks, six of which also took place in December (LICADHO, 2003: 5). The Tat Marina case stirred up great media attention as did the fact that the alleged perpetrator and accomplices were not arrested or sentenced. While it is possible that the number of cases of women burned has not increased and that it is just that the media has shown more interest in reporting each case, it is also possible that the Marina case contributed to the increase in attacks, in the sense that more people might think that throwing acid was not a crime that would be punished by law and would therefore end in impunity (LICADHO, 2003: 6). Concern that media coverage of these cases may lead to other acts of violence is also present in countries like Uganda (Acid Survivors' Foundation Uganda, 2011: 16).

In Spain, the risk of a possible copy-cat effect was brought into debate especially by forensic doctor Miguel Lorente, who stated that seeing a violent reality confirmed may encourage many perpetrators and fuel the fear that many abused women experience (Lorente, 2010: 19). Aware that men only consider homicide as a last resort, probably when violence does not have a controlling effect, he stated that seeing how another man had killed his wife in the media could reinforce his decision to commit the crime as he would be able to find aspects in common and identify with the feelings.

A study carried out in relation to media news on cases of intimate partner femicide in Spain allows us to identify a certain copy-cat effect when we compare the days when there [is] news on femicide cases and days that there [is] not. The conclusion is that televised news on cases of intimate partner femicides would appear to increase the possibility of death by femicide by between 32% and 42% (Vives, Torrubiano and Álvarez, 2009).

One case that proved the copy-cat effect in Latin America in recent years was the case of Wanda Taddei in Argentina. In Buenos Aires, on 10 February 2010, Wanda Taddei suffered serious burns caused by alcohol set alight by her husband, Eduardo Vázquez. She died after 11 days of agony and Vásquez remained at liberty until 4 November of the same year, because for months the justice believed his version that it was a domestic accident. On 14 June 2012, Eduardo Vásquez was sentenced to 18 years in prison for the crime.

The case had huge media coverage due to both the cruelty of the attack and because Eduardo Vázquez was a member of a rock band involved in a nightclub fire where nearly 200 people had died in 2004 for which all the band members were declared responsible and sentenced in 2012. As a result, the case was talked about extensively in news programmes and magazine shows.

According to the reports of the "La Casa del Encuentro" organisation, there has been an increase in the number of femicide cases in Argentina in recent years, reaching a peak in 2011.

Furthermore, the number of cases where women are set alight have become more common since 2010, when Wanda Taddei was murdered, rising from 2.6% of the total number of femicides in 2009 (6 women set alight) to reach 10.28% of cases in 2011 (29 women set alight).

Since Wanda Taddei's death in 2010 until the first half of 2013, 66 women have been burnt to death in Argentina. However, in addition to these cases of femicide, there have also been numerous cases of women attacked with fire: in the three years following the death of Wanda Taddei, 132 women were set on fire by men in Argentina, and nearly half of these women died.

By September 2010, women's organisations and some media were already warning about a repeat pattern in attacks on women and the far lower media interest in those other cases. Refererence to the "Wanda Taddei effect" is currently generalised at media level in Argentina to refer to the multiplication of femicide cases committed by burning since that case.

c) Increase of fear in women

The connection between violent narratives in the media and fear of crime has been studied in recent years and is the major focus of the cultivation theory (Morgan and Shanahan, 2010, cited by Custers and Van den Bluck, 2013: 99). The cultivation theory understands that the representation of crime and violence in the media may constitute a threat to democracy, as frightened peo-ple are more dependent, and more easily manipulated and controlled.

The media plays an important role in the level of fear of crime in general, and in particular in women. The press tends to over-represent women as victims (Greer, 2003; Reiner et at, 2003; Peelo et al, 2004, Custers and Van den Bluck, 2013) and homicides are more often reported in the press when the homicide victims are women (Peelo et al, 2004). News that focuses on the body of women who suffer gender-based violence is built on the concept of victims that need protection and assistance, and women from other cultures are linked to prostitution and gender-based violence (Martínez-Lirola, 2010, on CNTV, 2013: 25).

It is necessary to recognise that "violence against women and girls is both an extreme manifestation of gender inequality and discrimination and a deadly tool used to maintain women's subordinate status" (UN Women, 2011: 32). In this way, fear of becoming a victim of violence, often fuelled by the press, is a mechanism that contributes to ensuring the subordination of women.

d) Protective effect

The news has also been found to provide a protective effect when it focuses on initiatives against violence towards women and femicide (related to laws, statements from and interviews with politicians and key figures in the field of violence against women, or public acts that condemn this type of crime) instead of focusing on the crimes themselves. In the case of Spain, this effect was noted during the period when there was an increase in this type of news due to the passing of a new law on violence against women while the study was being carried out (Vives, Torrubiano and Álvarez, 2009).

Similarly, when the Law to Penalise Violence against Women was passed in 2007 in Costa Rica, there was a significant drop in the number of femicide cases, nearly half that of previous years, which can only be explained by the entry into force of the Law and the extensive media attention it received.

III. REGULATORY AND SELF-REGULATORY PROPOSALS

With regard to regulatory aspects, various international instruments – such as the Inter-American Convention on the Prevention, Punishment and Eradication of Violence against Women (Convention of Belem do Pará), the Beijing Declaration and its Platform for Action and the Convention of Istanbul, at [the] European level – have stressed the need for guidelines related to the treatment of violence against women in the media in order to contribute to its prevention and eradication.

In national legislation, however, laws do not expressly lay down how the media should address news on violence against women. In some laws regarding the press as well as in initiatives under discussion, there are related general provisions to prevent discriminatory content or content that incites discrimination based, among others, on gender. Additionally, some national laws on violence against women include general references to the role of the media.

The Spanish Law on Gender-based Violence has been more specific – possibly due to cases where the media has played a role in triggering attacks on women, and it states that "reports concerning violence against women, within the requirements of journalistic objectivity, shall do the utmost to defend human rights and the freedom and dignity of the female victims of gender violence and their children. In particular, they shall take special care in the graphic treatment of such items."

These regulations, however, do not impose direct obligations on the press which, under the principle of freedom of expression and press freedom, is subject only to the self-regulation of professional camera people, of business associations and specific media. In the case of Spain, for example, legal regulations have resulted in the creation of media observatories in some autonomous regions, news writing guidelines and recommendations on the treatment of gender-based violence in the media. These mechanisms depend, however, on the willingness of the media itself to apply the guidelines. For example, the annual reports of the Asociación de Mujeres Periodistas de Cataluña [Association of Women Journalists of Catalonia] show that the media persists in presenting cases of gender-based violence from a merely "informative" perspective, with little contextualising and an excessive use of adjectives that only seek to further dramatise the facts.

At [an] international level, various bodies have developed minimum standards to address the production of content and development of cultural industries from a gender perspective. In this regard, national and international guides have been prepared with suggestions on how to produce content with a gender perspective, to avoid stereotypes and to extend the type and number of specialised news sources that the media usually uses (IFJ, s/f; Alberti et al, 2010). There are also projects within the media itself that have driven gender policies, which include style guides (IPS, 2010; RTVE, 2002).

For example, in the case of Radio y Televisión Española, there is a full section with recommendations on how to cover issues related to violence against women. Among others, it includes respecting the victim's identity and pain, identifying the perpetrator, not confusing morbid curiosity with social interest, taking special care in the use of sources and the use of adjectives and providing useful information. In the case of Inter Press Service, a global news agency, it has a section specially dedicated to covering gender-based violence, as well as a style guide and a glossary of terms on gender, development and equity which now has various editions.

UNESCO has also promoted actions to encourage this debate and to implement actions on different levels, in association with various stakeholders. In December 2013, the Global Forum on Media Gender was held in Bangkok, as part of the Global Alliance for Media and Gender.

These tools, however, face some obstacles: they are often international, local or association regulations promoted without the participation of the media and/or media professionals, which leads to low level of uptake: compliance monitoring is non-existent or poor and they lack specific regulatory entities.

In terms of self-regulation, it is important to point out that the business associations that make up the media, for example, as well as professional journalist and communicators associations have formulated codes of news ethics and treatment. Furthermore, there are projects in relation to media or in particular media group style guides. In general, these refer to issues regarding sources, sensationalism, violence and sexual crimes and minimum standards (of the least damaging possible, for example, or respect to victims) which are relevant to covering violence against women and femicide (Taufic, 2004).

One of the problems of codes of ethics and style guides, however, is that in some countries these are not made public and have restricted access. Therefore, it is not possible to know the commitment of the media to its audience, thereby hindering the monitoring of the role of the media and journalists.

To the above-mentioned, we must add that various professional organisations and women's organisations have edited and promoted news coverage guides in these matters (Alberti et al, 2010; PAR, 2008; IJF, s/f). Nevertheless, the impact and specific application of the guides is unknown and depends on the culture of accountability of the media industry in each specific society, as well as its journalistic culture.

IV. CONCLUSIONS

Media coverage of violence against women and femicide/feminicide is one of a multiplicity of social factors that affect these phenomena. Although it is difficult to conclusively determine the extent of the effect or how it relates to other factors, its impact is nonetheless undeniable.

The studies analysed in this document at least enable us to establish that media coverage in these cases can have an impact on violence against women. This may occur in cases where, added to other factors, the media can influence potential perpetrators, women – the potential victims of violence – and society as a whole, through both male and female symbolic constructs as well as constructs regarding the relationships between men and women, thereby possibly contributing to consolidate a higher or lower tolerance to violence against women.

With regard to the obligations of states to prevent and eradicate violence against women, the influence of the media, even if it is relative, needs to be taken into consideration, and therefore the mechanisms that promote and favour appropriate information must be consolidated.

With regard to mass media, good practices need to be promoted that contribute to improving quality standards when covering violence against women, coherent with corporate social responsibility (CSR) policies which are slowly being incorporated at global level.

With regard to the press, journalists and communicators, high ethical and professional standards need to be put into practice when covering violence against women. For both the media and the press, these ethical, professional and social responsibility challenges need to be included in association and institutional instruments that provide guides to address this problem which, as we have seen, has an enormous impact on women's rights and public health at global level.

Even though these instruments such as legislation, guides, directives and guidelines exist to a greater or lesser extent in both Latin American and European countries, it is essential that they have the appropriate mechanisms to ensure their effectiveness. Communication channels and monitoring devices are necessary so that these frameworks first reach those who have to implement them, and then are complied with. This means that the media and press themselves have to be involved, both in their own specialist media and in their professional associations. Additionally, civil society actors can supervise the international and legal obligations and/or agreements examined here.

More progress is needed in the debate, formulation and dissemination of these types of legal (obligatory) or editorial and ethical guidelines. Finally, it is essential that the gender perspective, especially raising awareness of violence against women, is included in graduate and post-graduate journalism and communications courses. In these areas, however, there is still a long way to go.

1. How does media coverage impact violence against women?

2. What can be done to ensure media coverage does not have a negative impact on women's safety?

CHAPTER 2

WHAT THE GOVERNMENT AND POLITICIANS SAY

Lawmakers and government officials play an important role in shaping the way we confront and talk about sexual assault and gender violence. The laws that legislators pass dictate how we can hold perpetrators accountable, while the remarks made by presidents and other leaders make clear where we as a country stand on issues like harassment. Their role is complex; they respond to changing public understandings of what constitutes harassment or gender-based violence, while also impacting the way society responds to allegations of both. Some politicians choose to take on an active role in advocating for victims, while others show their support in other ways. These issues are also deeply political; foreign policy decisions can impact conflicts where gender violence takes place with greater frequency, and the allocation of funds as determined by federal budgets provides resources used to combat harassment in the workplace, on campuses, and in the military. But how best to confront these issues is hotly debated in the halls of government, as we will see in this chapter.

"REMARKS BY THE PRESIDENT AND VICE PRESIDENT AT AN EVENT FOR THE COUNCIL ON WOMEN AND GIRLS" BY FORMER PRESIDENT BARACK OBAMA AND FORMER VICE PRESIDENT JOSEPH BIDEN, FROM THE WHITE HOUSE ARCHIVES, JANUARY 22, 2014

THE VICE PRESIDENT: Folks, let me start off by telling you why I've never had a doubt about joining this man on the ticket and why I'm so proud of Valerie Jarrett and all that she does.

One of the first things the President did when we took office was set up the Council on Women and Girls because he believes with every fiber in his being, as I do, that his daughters and my granddaughters are entitled to every single, solitary opportunity my grandson and sons are entitled to – without a single exception.

And he established the Council on Women and Girls, and I appreciate the way Valerie and the council have embraced this mission. And I'm so proud to be working with you, Valerie. You've done an incredible job.

You've strengthened the Office of Violence Against Women, Mr. President, at the Department of the Justice. And I especially want to thank the President for appointing the first-ever Advisor on Violence Against Women working directly with me in the White House, inside this building.

He knows what I know: Freedom from sexual assault is a basic human right. No man has a right to raise a hand to a woman for any reason – any reason – other than self-defense. He knows that a nation's decency is in large part measured by how it responds to violence against women. He knows that our daughters, our sisters, our wives, our mothers, our grandmothers have every single right to expect to be free from violence and sexual abuse. No matter what she's wearing, no matter whether she's in a bar, in a dormitory, in the back seat of a car, on a street, drunk or sober, no man has a right to go beyond the word "No." And if she can't consent, it also means no. That too makes it a crime.

The President also knows that we have to stop blaming victims for these crimes. No one ever asks the person who got robbed at gunpoint in the street – why were you there, what were you doing, what were you wearing? What did you say? Did you offend someone? We encourage people to come forward. We don't have to explain why someone took our money.

My father used to say that the greatest abuse of all was the abuse of power, and the cardinal sin among the abuse of power avenues that can be taken is for a man to raise his hand to a woman. That's the cardinal sin. There's no justification, in addition, for us not intervening. Men have to step up to the bar here. Men have to take more responsibility. Men have to intervene. The measure of manhood is willingness to speak up and speak out, and begin to change the culture.

And so, ladies and gentlemen, I'd like to now introduce to the man who more than anyone I know – anyone I know – is wanting to change the environment for his daughters, my granddaughters, women and girls all across the United States of America. Like I said, it's stamped in his DNA, it's in his bloodstream, and we're lucky to have him leading us now – ladies and gentlemen, the President of the United States, Barack Obama. (Applause.)

THE PRESIDENT: Thank you. Thank you, everybody. (Applause.) Please have a seat. Hello, everybody. Welcome to the White House. To all of you in my administration – the partners with the White House Council on Women and Girls, led by Valerie and Tina Tchen – I want to thank all of you for being here today, and for the work that you're doing every single day to advance a cause that matters to all of us – and that's preventing the outrage, the crime, of sexual violence in America.

I especially want to thank the members of my Cabinet who are here today. We've got Secretaries Chuck Hagel, Kathleen Sebelius and Arne Duncan, as well as Attorney General Holder. And their presence here today, and the presence of so many leaders from across my adminis-tration, is a testament to how important we consider this issue and how committed we are across the entire federal government to meeting this challenge.

And that, of course, includes our outstanding Vice President. Few people have brought more passion to this fight over the decades than Joe Biden. Back when a lot of people believed that domestic abuse was a private family matter, and women in danger often had nobody to turn to, Joe was out there saying, "This is unacceptable. This has to change." And thanks to Joe and so many others, this nation enshrined its commitment in the Violence Against Women Act.

Police officers and prosecutors got special training on domestic violence. More shelters opened across the country. A national hotline was created. And as Joe mentioned, a cultural shift began to occur. Americans came to see how serious this problem was and how we all needed to do more to address it. And that's resulted in more hope and more safety and a new chance at life for countless women. So Joe is on the frontlines on this, and you can tell his passion is unabated. And so we are very grateful for everything that you've done on this work. Thank you, Joe. Appreciate it. (Applause.)

I think that conviction and that passion brings us all here today – because this is not an abstract problem that goes on in other families or other communities. Even now, it's not always talked about enough. It can still go on in the shadows. But it affects every one of us. It's about all of us – our moms, our wives, our sisters, our daughters, our sons. Sexual assault is an affront to our basic decency and humanity. And for survivors, the awful pain can take years, even decades to heal. Sometimes it lasts a lifetime. And wherever it occurs – whether it's in our neighborhoods or on our college campuses, our military bases or our tribal lands – it has to matter to all of us.

Because when a young girl or a young boy starts to question their self-worth after being assaulted, and maybe starts withdrawing, we're all deprived of their full potential. When a young woman drops out of school after being attacked, that's not just a loss for her, that's a loss for our country. We've all got a stake in that young woman's success.

When a mother struggles to hold down a job after a traumatic assault, or is assaulted in order to keep a job, that matters to all of us because strong families are a foundation of a strong country. And if that woman doesn't feel like she has recourse when she's subject to abuse, and we're not there supporting her, shame on us. When a member of our military is assaulted by the very people he or she trusted and serves with, or when they leave the military, voluntarily or involuntarily, because they were raped, that's a profound injustice that no one who volunteers to defend America should ever have to endure.

So sexual violence is more than just a crime against individuals. It threatens our families, it threatens our communities; ultimately, it threatens the entire country. It tears apart the fabric of our communities. And that's why we're here today – because we have the power to do something about it as a government, as a nation. We have the capacity to stop sexual assault, support those who have survived it, and bring perpetrators to justice. And that's why, last year, I was proud to sign the reauthorization of the Violence Against Women Act, which improved the support we gave to cities and states to help end sexual assault. And that includes funding to train police officers and nurses, and to speed up the processing of untested rape kits so we can reduce that backlog, solve unsolved cases, [and] get justice for victims.

We pushed for the Violence Against Women Act to include more protections for immigrants; for lesbian, gay, bisexual and transgender Americans; for Native Americans. Because no matter who you are or where you live, everybody in this country deserves security and justice and dignity. And we have to keep reaching out to people who are still suffering in the shadows.

As Commander-in-Chief, I've made it clear to our military leadership that we need to deal aggressively with the problem of sexual assault in our armed forces. It has been going on too long, and we have an obligation to protect the men and women who put their lives on the line to protect us. And Secretary Hagel and Chairman Dempsey have already taken steps to reduce violence and support those who have been harmed. But I've made it clear I expect significant progress in the year ahead. These crimes have no place in the greatest military on Earth.

I've directed agencies across the federal government to do more to help members of their workforce who have been assaulted – because employers have a role to play too, and I want my administration to lead by example. That's why we're releasing a new report today that outlines all of our efforts and where we intend to do more. And I met earlier today with Secretaries Sebelius, Hagel, Duncan, Attorney General Holder, as well as Vice President Biden, as well as members of my senior staff, to discuss how we implement going forward. Because I want to make sure we're doing everything we can to spare another American the trauma of sexual assault.

Today, we're taking another important step with a focus on our college campuses. It is estimated that 1 in 5 women on college campuses has been sexually assaulted during their time there – 1 in 5. These young women worked so hard just to get into college, often their parents are doing everything they can to help them pay for it. So when they finally make it there only to be assaulted, that is not just a nightmare for them and their families, it's an affront to everything they've worked so hard to achieve. It's totally unacceptable.

Three years ago, we sent every school district, college, and university that receives federal funding new instructions clarifying their legal obligations to prevent and respond to sexual assault. And we have seen progress, including an inspiring wave of student-led activism, and a growing number of students who found the courage to come forward and report attacks. That's exactly what we want them to do. And we owe all these brave young people an extraordinary debt of gratitude.

But we cannot stop there. There's obviously more that we have to do to keep our students safe. And that's why here today, I will sign a presidential memorandum creating the White House Task Force to Protect Students from Sexual Assault. And we're going to work with colleges and universities and educational institutions of all kinds across America to help them come up with better ways to prevent and respond to sexual assault on their campuses. And then we'll help them put those ideas into practice, because our schools need to be places where our young people feel secure and confident as they prepare to go as far as their God-given talents can carry them.

None of this is going to be easy. Some of you have worked on these issues for years. You know how long it took for our country to get to where we are now. And it didn't just take new laws. It took a fundamental change in our culture – a shift in our attitudes about how we think about sexual violence, and how much we value the lives and dignity of our wives and sisters and daughters and sons. And over time, we've become a better, stronger nation for it.

But now it's up to each of us – every single one of us – to keep up that momentum. We've got to keep teaching young men in particular to show women the respect they deserve and to recognize sexual violence and be outraged by it, and to do their part to stop it from happening in the first place. During our discussion earlier today, we talked about [how] I want every young man in America to feel some strong peer pressure in terms of how they are supposed to behave and treat women. And that starts before they get to college.

So those of us who are fathers have an obligation to transmit that information. But we can do more to make sure that every young man out there – whether they're in junior high or high school or college or beyond – understand[s] what's expected of them and what it means to be a man, and to intervene if they see somebody else acting inappropriately. We're going to need to encourage young people, men and women, to realize that sexual assault is simply unacceptable. And they're going to have to summon the bravery to stand up and say so, especially when the social pressure to keep quiet or to go along can be very intense.

We've got to keep working with our teachers and police officers and health professionals and community leaders to search for new ways to prevent these crimes. My hope and intention is, is that every college president who has not personally been thinking about this is going to hear about this report and is going to go out and figure out who is in charge on their campus of responding properly, and what are the best practices, and are we doing everything that we should be doing.

And if you're not doing that right now, I want the students at the school to ask the president what he is doing or she is doing. And perhaps most important, we need to keep saying to anyone out there who has ever been assaulted, you are not alone. You will never be alone. We have your back. I've got your back.

And I promise I'm going to keep fighting for you and your families, and I'm going to keep pushing for others to step up across my administration and in Congress, and in state capitals and college campuses and on our military bases and all across our country. This is a priority for me not only as President and Commander-in-Chief, but as a husband and a father of two extraordinary girls.

I've often said in my travels around the world: You can judge a nation, and how successful it will be, based on how it treats its women and its girls. Those nations that are successful, they're successful in part because women and girls are valued. And I'm determined that, by that measure, the United States of America will be the global leader. I'm grateful to each of you for making sure that happens. I'm grateful for Joe Biden for having led the charge both in Congress and in my administration on many of these issues.

1. What did the Obama administration do to confront sexual violence?

2. How do these measures position the United States in the global fight against sexual violence?

"IT'S ON US TO STOP CAMPUS SEXUAL ASSAULT" BY FORMER VICE PRESIDENT JOE BIDEN, FROM THE WHITE HOUSE ARCHIVES, NOVEMBER 9, 2015

Twenty-one years ago, I wrote the Violence Against Women Act to end the scourge of violence against women and hold perpetrators accountable. It's been a great success, but even one attack is one too many.

So I held a number of calls with hundreds of students, administrators, advocates, and survivors and asked what we can do to make colleges safer. The overwhelming answer – get men involved.

So President Obama and I started *It's On Us* to wake up our colleges and universities – and the country – to the epidemic of sexual violence on their campuses.

Over the past year, we've gotten celebrities, major companies, sports leagues, and leading broadcasters to participate in public service announcements and display logos and information showing how everyone can help prevent these heinous crimes from ever happening.

One thing students can do is take the *It's On Us* pledge. Over 250,000 students have already pledged:

1. To intervene instead of being a bystander.

2. To recognize that any time consent is not – or cannot – be given, it is sexual assault and it is a crime.

3. To do everything you can to create an environment where sexual assault is unacceptable, and all survivors are supported.

The response has been overwhelming. More than 300 campuses have hosted over 1,000 *It's On Us* events, and nearly 300 colleges and universities have created their own *It's On Us* public service announcements, reaching millions of people online and at football and basketball games.

But this year, we want to do even more. That's why between November 8th to November 14th, I'm traveling across the country calling for a Week of Action to get more students involved.

This week, the University of Wisconsin is hosting an It's On Us flag football game with student athletes, members of Greek organizations, and other student groups. At Stonehill College in Massachusetts, students, faculty, and staff are wearing nametags that say how they have been affected by sexual assault: "I am a survivor," and "I will not be a passive bystander." Middle Tennessee State University is hosting discussions in the student center and online about consent and stopping sexual violence.

In addition to taking the pledge, consider other steps:

- Organize drives to get more students to take the *It's On Us* Pledge.
- Ask businesses, libraries, [and] hospitals to display an *It's On Us* logo.
- Encourage sports teams, fraternities, sororities, bands, and other student organizations to get involved.
- Hold press conferences and roundtables with school administrators and community leaders about campus sexual assault.
- Use social media to spread the word using #ItsOnUs.

You have to demand that your Universities be held accountable. President Obama and I have made it crystal clear that schools that fail in this responsibility are in violation of Title IX and risk federal investigation and financial penalties. And each of you can make it clear that you expect nothing less.

I also encourage your colleges to partner with local rape crisis centers, local law enforcement, and women's health centers to coordinate a robust community response and ensure that victims are supported in every way possible.

We have more to do to change the culture that asks the wrong questions, like why were you there? What were you wearing? Were you drinking?

We have to ask the right questions – What made him think that he could do what he did without my consent? Why on Earth did no one stop him instead of standing by? What can we do to make sure everyone has the courage to speak up, intervene, prevent and end sexual assault once and for all?

You know that survivors are not statistics. They're our sisters; they're our classmates; they're our friends. They're at every university, every college, in every community – large and small. For all of them, everywhere, we can and we must end sexual and dating violence on campus.

But we can't do it without you. Visit www.itsonus.org to find out what you can do during this Week of Action and throughout the school year.

It's on me. It's on you. It's on us – and it's within our power to end sexual violence on campus once and for all.

1. What actions does the *It's On Us* campaign ask people to take?

2. How can college students change the rates of sexual harassment on campus?

"REMARKS BY SENATOR JOHN MCCAIN ON THE IMAGINARY 'WAR ON WOMEN' ON THE FLOOR OF THE US SENATE" BY JOHN MCCAIN, FROM *JOHN MCCAIN—US SENATOR—ARIZONA*, APRIL 26, 2012

Mr. President, I rise today to discuss the Violence Against Women Act and policies that impact the lives of women.

Since its original enactment in 1994, the Violence Against Women Act has been reauthorized twice by unanimous consent under both Democrat and Republican Leadership. The legislation originated out of a necessity for us to respond to the prevalence of domestic violence, sexual violence and the impact those crimes have on the lives of women. By and large, the legislation has worked, even though there are outstanding issues like spending inefficiencies and needed improvements to oversight. As with most large pieces of legislation, including the Violence Against Women Act reauthorization before us today, there are debates and philosophical differences about elements of various provisions in the bill. And while the Senate should be allowed to debate and, ideally, resolve those differences, I don't think any of the points of controversy we will discuss today are important enough to prevent passage of this legislation. The Violence Against Women Act represents a national commitment to reversing the legacy of laws and social norms that once served to shamefully excuse violence towards women, a commitment that should be maintained.

Whatever differences we might have over particular provisions in the bill, surely we are united in our concern for the victims of violence and our determination to do all that we can to prevent violence against the innocent, regardless of gender. I recognize that women suffer disproportionately from particular forms of violence and other abuse, which this legislation is intended to address, and, I believe, does address, which is why I support it. But our motivation to act on their behalf resides in our respect for the rights all human beings possess, male and female, all races, creeds and ages, to be secure in their persons and property, to be protected by their government from violent harm at the hands of another, to live without threat or fear in the exercise of their God-given rights.

Similarly, whatever our political differences in this body, I trust we all believe we are doing what we think best serves the interests and values of the American people, all of the American people. I don't think either party is entitled to speak or act exclusively for one demographic of our population, one class, one race or one gender. The security and prosperity of all Americans is a shared responsibility, and each of us discharges it to the best of our ability. We don't have male and female political parties, and we don't need to accuse each other of caring less for the concerns of one half of the population than we do for the other half.

The truth is both parties have presided over achievements and increases in opportunit[ies] for women. Both parties have nominated women to the Supreme Court. Both parties have had excellent female Secretaries of State. Both parties have had female Presidential and Vice Presidential candidates. Both parties have reauthorized the Violence Against Women Act. Both parties have made progress toward ensuring [that] Americans, male and female, have an equal opportunity to succeed as far as their talents and industry can take them. That progress has come in the form of many policies; from changes to our tax code to changes in education policy to improvements in workplace environments, as well as from changes in cultural attitudes in both the public and private sector. Do we always agree? Do we always get it right? No, we don't. But I do think there is much for all of us to be proud of.

Regrettably – and there is always something to regret in politics – we have seen too many attempts to resolve inequities in our society and ensure all Americans are afforded the same respect for their rights and aspirations misappropriated for the purpose of partisan advantage, which has the perverse effect, of course, of dividing the country in the name of greater fairness and unity.

My friends, this supposed 'War on Women' or the use of similarly outlandish rhetoric by partisan operatives has two purposes, and both are purely political in their purpose and effect. The first is to distract citizens from real issues that really matter and the second is to give talking heads something to sputter about when they appear on cable television. Neither purpose does anything to advance the well being of any American.

Mr. President, I've been fortunate to be influenced throughout my life by the example of strong, independent, aspiring and caring women. As a son, brother, husband, father and grandfather, I think I can claim some familiarity with the contributions women make to the health and progress of our society. I can certainly speak to their beneficial impact on my life and character. But I would never claim to speak for all the women in my family, much less all the women in our country, any more than I would venture the same presumption for all men. To suggest that one group of us or one party speaks for all women or that one group has an agenda to harm women and another to help them is ridiculous. If for no other reason than it assumes a unity of interests, beliefs, concerns, experiences and ambitions among all women that doesn't exist among men or among any race or class. It would be absurd for me to speak for all veterans, and wrong of me to suggest that if a colleague who isn't a veteran disagrees with my opinion on some issue, he or she must be against all of our veterans.

In America, all we can fairly claim to have in common with each other at all times, no matter what gender we are or what demographic we fit, are our rights. As a son, brother, husband, father and grandfather, I have the same dreams and concerns for all the people in my life. As a public servant, I have the same respect for their rights, and the same responsibility to protect them, and I try to do so to the best of my ability.

Thankfully, I believe women and men in our country are smart enough to recognize that when a politician or political party resorts to dividing us in the name of bringing us together it usually means that they are either out of ideas or short on resolve to address the challenges of our time. At this time in our nation's history, we face an abundance of hard choices. Divisive slogans and the declaring of phony wars are intended to avoid those hard choices and to escape paying a political price for doing so.

For 38 straight months our unemployment rate has been over 8 percent. Millions of Americans – women and men – cannot find a job and many have quit looking. Americans don't need another hollow slogan or another call to division and partisanship. They need real solutions to their problems. They are desperate for them.

Americans of both genders are concerned about finding and keeping a good job. Americans of both genders are concerned about the direction of our economy. Women and men are concerned about mounting debt, their own and the nation's. Women and men are hurt by high gas prices, by the housing crisis, shrinking wages, [and] the cost of health care. Women and men are concerned about their children's security, their education, [and] their prospects for inheriting an America that offers every mother and father's child a decent chance at reaching their full potential. Leaving these problems unaddressed indefinitely and resorting to provoking greater divisions among us at a time when we most need unity might not be a war against this or that group of Americans – but it is surely a surrender; a surrender of our responsibilities to the country and a surrender of decency.

Mr. President, within the tired suggestions that women are singularly focused on one or two issues are the echoes of stale arguments from the past. Women are as variable in their opinions and concerns as men. Those false assertions are rooted in the past stereotypes that prevented women from becoming whatever they wanted to become, which slowed our progress and hurt our country in many ways. The argument is as wrong now as it was then. And we ought not repeat it.

We have only these in common: our equal right to the pursuit of happiness, and our shared responsibility to making America an even better place than we found it. Women and men are no different in their rights and responsibilities. I believe this legislation recognizes that. I don't believe the ludicrous, partisan posturing that has conjured up this imaginary war.

Thank you.

1. What is Senator McCain arguing against in this speech?

2. What are the solutions he puts forward to get past politics and combat violence against women?

"GOVERNMENT SLOW TO RESPOND TO EPIDEMIC OF SEXUAL ASSAULTS" BY CAITLIN CRUZ AND ASHA ANCHAN, FROM *NEWS21*, AUGUST 24, 2013

At least one in five female veterans of the wars in Iraq and Afghanistan has screened positive for military sexual trauma (MST) once back home, Department of Veterans Affairs records show. And this may understate the crisis, experts say, because this number only counts women who go to the VA for help.

Young female veterans — those returning from the wars in Iraq and Afghanistan — often don't show up for their first VA appointments, if they show up at all, said Ann LeFevre, MST coordinator at the VA Palo Alto Health Care System in California. "They think they're alone and they don't want to talk about it," LeFevre said. "Especially with new returners, it takes a lot to get them on the VA campus. It can remind them of their base where the assault occurred."

The assault itself defies the discipline and values of the armed forces, but the problem is exacerbated, experts say, when victims report an assault and their allegations are met with skepticism and possible retaliation.

Even after their military service is over, many sexual assault victims are reluctant to approach the VA, a system intertwined with the military and perceived at times as prescribing drugs instead of meeting their treatment needs.

"There's a disconnect between what survivors believe they need and the educated treatment community as to what is necessary and helpful," said Mylea Charvat, a fellow in clinical neuroscience with the Stanford School of Medicine.

Charvat, who worked in the VA system for about 10 years, starting shortly after 9/11, described the department as "slow to respond" to the broad needs of women. "Historically, it's not a highly responsive system. It's huge, it's bureaucratic," she said. "I can understand women being hesitant to seek care, and frankly, a lot of men, too."

In 2012, the Department of Defense's Sexual Assault Prevention and Response Office estimated that 26,000 cases of "unwanted sexual contact" occurred. Of these, only about 13 percent of service members reported their assault.

Now, Charvat is working to develop a new model for effectively treating military sexual trauma and the resulting post-traumatic stress disorder with the Artemis Rising Invisible War Recovery Program, a treatment program inspired by the documentary "The Invisible War."

"We need to attack this [with] a multi-faceted approach," she said. "It's a complex problem."

The burden of the problem falls on the Department of Defense — which consistently states it has a zero-tolerance policy for sexual assault — and on the VA — which has been charged since 1992 with addressing the failures of that policy. In 2010, the VA spent $872 million on sexual-assault-related healthcare, records show.

But many veterans feel lost in the void between these two large bureaucracies.

Women like Jessie de Leon and Corey Barrows are veterans who feel the military failed them — not only because the assaults occurred, but also because of what they consider inadequate responses once they returned from their deployments. As a result, they sought their own means of treatment.

"For a while it's just like I was numb to the world. Just fake happiness, drug-induced happiness," said de Leon, who reported being raped while serving as an Army medic in Bamberg, Germany, from 2007 to 2009. "I didn't realize that this process was going to be more hindering to me in trying to recover from it than it was helping me."

As a medic, she examined soldiers and their families at the health clinic in Germany and prepared soldiers to be deployed to Iraq and Afghanistan. She also comforted families who lost soldiers in the war.

But back home in Florida, de Leon found no comfort with therapists at the West Palm Beach VA. They didn't seem to understand the impact of her rape. Their recommended treatment consisted of prescription drugs for sleeping, anxiety and depression.

Harvard psychologist Paula Caplan has talked with hundreds of veterans, many of whom told her the VA pushed prescription drugs instead of examining the impact of the assaults.

"Women already, so often, feel that they don't belong in the military, either they're not wanted or they have to prove to other people or themselves that they deserve to be there," Caplan said. "When you are traumatized and you're devastated ... then you think, 'But I have military training, I'm supposed to be tough, I'm supposed to be resilient.'"

De Leon had a young son, she was going to nursing school and she decided to leave the VA. Eventually, de Leon ended up at Healing Horse Therapy Center with other female veterans, located in Loxahatchee, Fla., 15 minutes from her home.

"No one was forcing you to talk, nobody was saying you had to do anything," de Leon said of the therapy center. "I didn't realize you could gain so much confidence, gain so much self-motivation, get back your self-esteem, just by working with a horse, who never said a word to you."

In October, she will graduate from nursing school and she and her 5-year-old son will move to North Carolina to be with her fiance.

"From going through years of a lot of people not caring about what you went through and how you felt about things, and to finally come to a place where you felt safe, it was, it was very wonderful," she said. "It validates your pain."

The VA defines military sexual trauma, or MST, as the "psychological trauma, which in the judgment of a VA mental health professional, resulted from a physical assault of a sexual nature, battery of a sexual nature, or sexual harassment which occurred while the veteran was serving on active duty or active duty for training."

Veterans can seek a disability compensation rating for MST and the related effects. According to the VA, the necessary documentation has been reduced. Despite this, Amanda Schroeder, a union president for employees of the Veterans Benefits Administration in Portland, Ore., said MST claims are complicated and time-consuming to complete because many people do not report their assault.

"Men and women alike are already completely disabused, disempowered and often completely disenfranchised by the time they get to us and so a lot of times the sexual trauma cases take a lot of time because we have to seek so much additional evidence and it's not all maintained in one place," Schroeder said.

Because of this, Rep. Chellie Pingree, D-Maine, introduced the 2013 Ruth Moore Act, which aims to make it easier for service members to receive benefits for military-related sexual assaults.

"Most people are just shocked to think that we would ask someone to serve in the military and they would be more likely to be sexually assaulted than blown up by an IED (improvised explosive device)," she said.

Pingree said her bill, which passed the House and is pending in the Senate, is needed because of the difficulty she's seen when victims try to prove they were sexually assaulted. "You can't just say to someone, 'Come serve your country, and oh, by the way, you might get raped if you do and we're not going to do anything about it,'" Pingree said. "It's just unthinkable."

In January, Army Gen. Martin Dempsey, the chairman of the Joint Chiefs of Staff, said he believes sexual assault and harassment continue "because we've had separate classes of military personnel." Identifying men as "warriors" and women as "something else" breeds an environment that can lead to sexual crimes, he said.

A 2013 Institute of Medicine report found a link between MST and long-term poor mental and physical health. Moreover, the Independent Budget, a policy evaluation created by various veteran service organizations about, but independent of, the VA, found that women with MST had a 59 percent higher risk for mental health problems.

Common conditions linked to MST range from PTSD and anxiety to eating disorders, hypervigilance and insomnia. More specifically, LaFevre said the women she works with often show signs of stomach problems, experience weight gain — "They don't want to get attention from men in any way, so they emotionally eat" — and have a hard time maintaining a job, leading to homelessness. The Independent Budget reported that of homeless female veterans using VA healthcare, 39 percent screened positive for MST.

These side effects remain wide-ranging and lifelong and the resources for treatment vary across the country.

"The assault itself is very traumatizing," said Jennifer Norris, an advocate with the Military Rape Crisis Center who was assaulted while serving with the Air Force and Air National Guard. "That trauma, you're going to have it no matter what, for the rest of your life."

Marine Corps veteran Corey Barrows reported that she was raped by a fellow service member while off-post in September 2006, near Marine Corps Air Station Cherry Point, N.C. When she reported her assault, her master sergeant told her she must have been too drunk — even though she doesn't drink. "Nobody believed me," she said.

She deployed in July 2007 to Iraq, where she was coping with her trauma — until her old unit, which included friends of her attacker, deployed to the same installation.

"We talk so much about unit cohesion being critically important in the military, just how well people work together when they're serving, and it's hard to imagine that anything does more damage to that than a sexual assault within a unit," said Pingree, the congresswoman from Maine. "It's not good policy to let it happen."

Barrows was honorably discharged in November 2008. After enrolling in VA healthcare in early 2009, she was prescribed numerous medications for anxiety and depression. She then went to a civilian therapist because she had lost faith in the VA system. Her therapist suggested activities such as yoga and talking with other survivors to aid Barrows's recovery. Barrows now uses fewer medications.

After her husband was discharged from the Marine Corps, they moved to his hometown of Bozeman, Mont.

"It's just therapeutic out here. I'm out of the military bubble," she said. "I still have horrible anxiety, especially with crowds, but in Montana you tend to have less of that."

1. What are a few of the obstacles standing in the way of efforts to stop military sexual assault?

2. What are the long-term effects of harassment and gender violence in the military?

CHAPTER 3

WHAT THE COURTS SAY

Lawsuits around the country concerning sexual harassment or assault are fairly common, but those that move the needle of public understanding and how we address issues of harassment and gender violence are rare. It was in 1986 when sexual harassment was found to be in violation of the Civil Rights Act of 1964, a groundbreaking case that is featured in this chapter. Courts also hear cases on how funds are allocated to help people vulnerable to sexual violence, as seen in this chapter in *Booth v. Hvass*. Cases like these are important because they shape the way laws are formed and the way we as a country consider discrimination or violence based on gender. The rationale for cases like these, both in terms of why they were filed and why the court ruled as they did, is also important; it offers a glimpse into how laws can impact wide-ranging issues and how their interpretation can change with time.

EXCERPT FROM "UNITED STATES SUPREME COURT: *MERITOR SAVINGS BANK V. VINSON,* (1986) NO. 84-1979" FROM THE UNITED STATES SUPREME COURT, JUNE 19, 1986

I

In 1974, respondent Mechelle Vinson met Sidney Taylor, a vice president of what is now petitioner Meritor Savings Bank (bank) and manager of one of its branch offices. When respondent asked whether she might obtain employment at the bank, Taylor gave her an application, which she completed and returned the next day; later that same day Taylor called her to say that she had been hired. With Taylor as her supervisor, respondent started as a teller-trainee, and thereafter was promoted to teller, head teller, and assistant [477 U.S. 57, 60] branch manager. She worked at the same branch for four years, and it is undisputed that her advancement there was based on merit alone. In September 1978, respondent notified Taylor that she was taking sick leave for an indefinite period. On November 1, 1978, the bank discharged her for excessive use of that leave.

Respondent brought this action against Taylor and the bank, claiming that during her four years at the bank she had "constantly been subjected to sexual harassment" by Taylor in violation of Title VII. She sought injunctive relief, compensatory and punitive damages against Taylor and the bank, and attorney's fees.

At the 11-day bench trial, the parties presented conflicting testimony about Taylor's behavior during respondent's employment. Respondent testified that during her probationary period as a teller-trainee, Taylor treated her in a fatherly way and made no sexual advances. Shortly thereafter, however, he invited her out to dinner and, during the course of the meal, suggested that they go to a motel to have sexual relations. At first she refused, but out of what she described as fear of losing her job she eventually agreed. According to respondent, Taylor thereafter made repeated demands upon her for sexual favors, usually at the branch, both during and after business hours; she estimated that over the next several years she had intercourse with him some 40 or 50 times. In addition, respondent testified that Taylor fondled her in front of other employees, followed her into the women's restroom when she went there alone, exposed himself to her, and even forcibly raped her on several occasions. These activities ceased after 1977, respondent stated, when she started going with a steady boyfriend.

Respondent also testified that Taylor touched and fondled other women employees of the bank, and she attempted to [477 U.S. 57, 61] call witnesses to support this charge. But while some supporting testimony apparently was admitted without objection, the District Court did not allow her "to present wholesale evidence of a pattern and practice relating to sexual advances to other female employees in her case in chief, but advised her that she might well be able to present such evidence in rebuttal to the defendants' cases." Vinson v. Taylor, 22 EPD § 30,708, p. 14,693, n. 1, 23 FEP Cases 37, 38-39, n. 1 (DC 1980). Respondent did not offer such evidence in rebuttal. Finally, respondent testified that because she was afraid of Taylor she never reported his harassment to any of his supervisors and never attempted to use the bank's complaint procedure.

Taylor denied respondent's allegations of sexual activity, testifying that he never fondled her, never made suggestive remarks to her, never engaged in sexual intercourse with her, and never asked her to do so. He contended instead that respondent made her accusations in response to a business-related dispute. The bank also denied respondent's allegations and asserted that any sexual harassment by Taylor was unknown to the bank and engaged in without its consent or approval.

The District Court denied relief, but did not resolve the conflicting testimony about the existence of a sexual relationship between respondent and Taylor. It found instead that

> "[i]f [respondent] and Taylor did engage in an intimate or sexual relationship during the time of [respondent's] employment with [the bank], that relationship was a voluntary one having nothing to do with her continued employment at [the bank] or her advancement or promotions at that institution." Id., at 14,692, 23 FEP Cases, at 42 (footnote omitted).

The court ultimately found that respondent "was not the victim of sexual harassment and was not the victim of sexual discrimination" while employed at the bank. Ibid., 23 FEP Cases, at 43. [477 U.S. 57, 62]

Although it concluded that respondent had not proved a violation of Title VII, the District Court nevertheless went on to address the bank's liability. After noting the bank's express policy against discrimination, and finding that neither respondent nor any other employee had ever lodged a complaint about sexual harassment by Taylor, the court ultimately concluded that "the bank was without notice and cannot be held liable for the alleged actions of Taylor." Id., at 14,691, 23 FEP Cases, at 42.

The Court of Appeals for the District of Columbia Circuit reversed. 243 U.S. App. D.C. 323, 753 F.2d 141 (1985). Relying on its earlier holding in Bundy v. Jackson, 205 U.S. App. D.C. 444, 641 F.2d 934 (1981), decided after the trial in this case, the court stated that a violation of Title VII may be predicated on either of two types of sexual harassment: harassment that involves the conditioning of concrete employment benefits on sexual favors, and harassment that, while not affecting economic benefits, creates a hostile or offensive working environment. The court drew additional support for this position from the Equal Employment Opportunity Commission's Guidelines on Discrimination Because of Sex, 29 CFR 1604.11(a) (1985), which set out these two types of sexual harassment claims. Believing that "Vinson's grievance was clearly of the [hostile environment] type," 243 U.S. App. D.C., at 327, 753 F.2d, at 145, and that the District Court had not considered whether a violation of this type had occurred, the court concluded that a remand was necessary.

The court further concluded that the District Court's finding that any sexual relationship between respondent and Taylor "was a voluntary one" did not obviate the need for a remand. "[U]ncertain as to precisely what the [district] court meant" by this finding, the Court of Appeals held that if the evidence otherwise showed that "Taylor made Vinson's toleration of sexual harassment a condition of her employment," her voluntariness "had no materiality whatsoever." [477 U.S. 57, 63]   Id., at 328, 753 F.2d, at 146. The court then surmised that the District Court's finding of voluntariness might have been based on "the voluminous testimony regarding respondent's dress and personal fantasies," testimony that the Court of Appeals believed "had no place in this litigation." Id., at 328, n. 36, 753 F.2d, at 146, n. 36.

As to the bank's liability, the Court of Appeals held that an employer is absolutely liable for sexual harassment practiced by supervisory personnel, whether or not the employer knew or should have known about the misconduct. The court relied chiefly on Title VII's definition of "employer" to include "any agent of such a person," 42 U.S.C. 2000e(b), as well as on the EEOC Guidelines. The court held that a supervisor is an "agent" of his employer for Title VII purposes, even if he lacks authority to hire, fire, or promote, since "the mere existence – or even the appearance – of a significant degree of influence in vital job decisions gives any supervisor the opportunity to impose on employees." 243 U.S. App. D.C., at 332, 753 F.2d, at 150.

In accordance with the foregoing, the Court of Appeals reversed the judgment of the District Court and remanded the case for further proceedings. A subsequent suggestion for rehearing en banc was denied, with three judges dissenting. 245 U.S. App. D.C. 306, 760 F.2d 1330 (1985). We granted certiorari, 474 U.S. 1047(1985), and now affirm but for different reasons.

II

Title VII of the Civil Rights Act of 1964 makes it "an unlawful employment practice for an employer . . . to discriminate against any individual with respect to his compensation, terms, conditions, or privileges of employment, because of such individual's race, color, religion, sex, or national origin." 42 U.S.C. 2000e-2(a)(1). The prohibition against discrimination based on sex was added to Title VII at the last minute on the floor of the House of Representatives. 110 Cong. Rec. 2577-2584 (1964). The principal argument in opposition [477 U.S. 57, 64] to the amendment was that "sex discrimination" was sufficiently different from other types of discrimination that it ought to receive separate legislative treatment. See id., at 2577 (statement of Rep. Celler quoting letter from United States Department of Labor); id., at 2584 (statement of Rep. Green). This argument was defeated, the bill quickly passed as amended, and we are left with little legislative history to guide us in interpreting the Act's prohibition against discrimination based on "sex."

Respondent argues, and the Court of Appeals held, that unwelcome sexual advances that create an offensive or hostile working environment violate Title VII. Without question, when a supervisor sexually harasses a subordinate because of the subordinate's sex, that supervisor "discriminate[s]" on the basis of sex. Petitioner apparently does not challenge this proposition. It contends instead that in prohibiting discrimination with respect to "compensation, terms, conditions, or privileges" of employment, Congress was concerned with what petitioner describes as "tangible loss" of "an economic character," not "purely psychological aspects of the workplace environment." Brief for Petitioner 30-31, 34. In support of this claim petitioner observes that in both the legislative history of Title VII and this Court's Title VII decisions, the focus has been on tangible, economic barriers erected by discrimination.

We reject petitioner's view. First, the language of Title VII is not limited to "economic" or "tangible" discrimination. The phrase "terms, conditions, or privileges of employment" evinces a congressional intent "to strike at the entire spectrum of disparate treatment of men and women" in employment. Los Angeles Dept. of Water and

Power v. Manhart, 435 U.S. 702, 707 , n. 13 (1978), quoting Sprogis v. United Air Lines, Inc., 444 F.2d 1194, 1198 (CA7 1971). Petitioner has pointed to nothing in the Act to suggest that Congress contemplated the limitation urged here. [477 U.S. 57, 65]

Second, in 1980 the EEOC issued Guidelines specifying that "sexual harassment," as there defined, is a form of sex discrimination prohibited by Title VII. As an "administrative interpretation of the Act by the enforcing agency," Griggs v. Duke Power Co., 401 U.S. 424, 433 -434 (1971), these Guidelines, "while not controlling upon the courts by reason of their authority, do constitute a body of experience and informed judgment to which courts and litigants may properly resort for guidance," General Electric Co. v. Gilbert, 429 U.S. 125, 141 -142 (1976), quoting Skidmore v. Swift & Co., 323 U.S. 134, 140 (1944). The EEOC Guidelines fully support the view that harassment leading to noneconomic injury can violate Title VII.

In defining "sexual harassment," the Guidelines first describe the kinds of workplace conduct that may be actionable under Title VII. These include "[u]nwelcome sexual advances, requests for sexual favors, and other verbal or physical conduct of a sexual nature." 29 CFR 1604.11(a) (1985). Relevant to the charges at issue in this case, the Guidelines provide that such sexual misconduct constitutes prohibited "sexual harassment," whether or not it is directly linked to the grant or denial of an economic quid pro quo, where "such conduct has the purpose or effect of unreasonably interfering with an individual's work performance or creating an intimidating, hostile, or offensive working environment." 1604.11(a)(3).

In concluding that so-called "hostile environment"

(i.e., non quid pro quo) harassment violates Title VII, the EEOC drew upon a substantial body of judicial decisions and EEOC precedent holding that Title VII affords employees the right to work in an environment free from discriminatory intimidation, ridicule, and insult. See generally 45 Fed. Reg. 74676 (1980). Rogers v. EEOC, 454 F.2d 234 (CA5 1971), cert. denied, 406 U.S. 957 (1972), was apparently the first case to recognize a cause of action based upon a discriminatory work environment. In Rogers, the Court of Appeals for the Fifth [477 U.S. 57, 66] Circuit held that a Hispanic complainant could establish a Title VII violation by demonstrating that her employer created an offensive work environment for employees by giving discriminatory service to its Hispanic clientele. The court explained that an employee's protections under Title VII extend beyond the economic aspects of employment:

> "[T]he phrase 'terms, conditions or privileges of employment' in [Title VII] is an expansive concept which sweeps within its protective ambit the practice of creating a working environment heavily charged with ethnic or racial discrimination. . . . One can readily envision working environments so heavily polluted with discrimination as to destroy completely the emotional and psychological stability of minority group workers . . . ." 454 F.2d, at 238.

Courts applied this principle to harassment based on race, e. g., Firefighters Institute for Racial Equality v. St. Louis, 549 F.2d 506, 514-515 (CA8), cert. denied sub nom. Banta v. United States, 434 U.S. 819 (1977); Gray v. Greyhound Lines, East, 178 U.S. App. D.C. 91, 98, 545 F.2d 169, 176 (1976), religion, e. g., Compston v. Borden, Inc.,

424 F. Supp. 157 (SD Ohio 1976), and national origin, e. g., Cariddi v. Kansas City Chiefs Football Club, 568 F.2d 87, 88 (CA8 1977). Nothing in Title VII suggests that a hostile environment based on discriminatory sexual harassment should not be likewise prohibited. The Guidelines thus appropriately drew from, and were fully consistent with, the existing case law.

Since the Guidelines were issued, courts have uniformly held, and we agree, that a plaintiff may establish a violation of Title VII by proving that discrimination based on sex has created a hostile or abusive work environment. As the Court of Appeals for the Eleventh Circuit wrote in Henson v. Dundee, 682 F.2d 897, 902 (1982): [477 U.S. 57, 67]

> "Sexual harassment which creates a hostile or offensive environment for members of one sex is every bit the arbitrary barrier to sexual equality at the workplace that racial harassment is to racial equality. Surely, a requirement that a man or woman run a gauntlet of sexual abuse in return for the privilege of being allowed to work and make a living can be as demeaning and disconcerting as the harshest of racial epithets."

Accord, Katz v. Dole, 709 F.2d 251, 254-255 (CA4 1983); Bundy v. Jackson, 205 U.S. App. D.C., at 444-454, 641 F.2d, at 934-944; Zabkowicz v. West Bend Co., 589 F. Supp. 780 (ED Wis. 1984).

Of course, as the courts in both Rogers and Henson recognized, not all workplace conduct that may be described as "harassment" affects a "term, condition, or privilege" of employment within the meaning of Title VII. See Rogers v. EEOC, supra, at 238 ("mere utterance of an ethnic or racial epithet which engenders offensive feelings in an employee" would not affect the conditions of employment to [a] sufficiently significant degree to violate Title VII); Henson, 682 F.2d, at 904 (quoting same). For sexual harassment to be actionable, it must be sufficiently severe or pervasive "to alter the conditions of [the victim's] employment and create an abusive working environment." Ibid. Respondent's allegations in this case – which include not only pervasive harassment but also criminal conduct of the most serious nature – are plainly sufficient to state a claim for "hostile environment" sexual harassment.

The question remains, however, whether the District Court's ultimate finding that respondent "was not the victim of sexual harassment," 22 EPD § 30,708, at 14,692-14,693, 23 FEP Cases, at 43, effectively disposed of respondent's claim. The Court of Appeals recognized, we think correctly, that this ultimate finding was likely based on one or both of two erroneous views of the law. First, the District Court apparently believed that a claim for sexual harassment will not lie [477 U.S. 57, 68] absent an economic effect on the complainant's employment. See ibid. ("It is without question that sexual harassment of female employees in which they are asked or required to submit to sexual demands as a condition to obtain employment or to maintain employment or to obtain promotions falls within protection of Title VII.") Since it appears that the District Court made its findings without ever considering the "hostile environment" theory of sexual harassment, the Court of Appeals' decision to remand was correct.

Second, the District Court's conclusion that no actionable harassment occurred might have rested on its earlier "finding" that "[i]f [respondent] and Taylor did engage in an intimate or sexual relationship . . . that relationship was a voluntary one." Id., at 14,692, 23 FEP Cases, at 42. But the fact that sex-related conduct was "voluntary," in the sense that the complainant was not forced to participate against her will, is not a defense to a sexual harassment suit brought under Title VII. The gravamen of any sexual harassment claim is that the alleged sexual advances were "unwelcome." 29 CFR 1604.11(a) (1985). While the question whether particular conduct was indeed unwelcome presents difficult problems of proof and turns largely on credibility determinations committed to the trier of fact, the District Court in this case erroneously focused on the "voluntariness" of respondent's participation in the claimed sexual episodes. The correct inquiry is whether respondent by her conduct indicated that the alleged sexual advances were unwelcome, not whether her actual participation in sexual intercourse was voluntary.

Petitioner contends that even if this case must be remanded to the District Court, the Court of Appeals erred in one of the terms of its remand. Specifically, the Court of Appeals stated that testimony about respondent's "dress and personal fantasies," 243 U.S. App. D.C., at 328, n. 36, 753 F.2d, at 146, n. 36, which the District Court apparently admitted [477 U.S. 57, 69] into evidence, "had no place in this litigation." Ibid. The apparent ground for this conclusion was that respondent's voluntariness vel non in submitting to Taylor's advances was immaterial to her sexual harassment claim. While "voluntariness" in the sense of consent is not a defense to such a claim, it does not follow that a complainant's sexually provocative speech or dress is irrelevant as a matter of law in determining whether he or she found particular sexual advances unwelcome. To the contrary, such evidence is obviously relevant. The EEOC

Guidelines emphasize that the trier of fact must determine the existence of sexual harassment in light of "the record as a whole" and "the totality of circumstances, such as the nature of the sexual advances and the context in which the alleged incidents occurred." 29 CFR 1604.11(b) (1985). Respondent's claim that any marginal relevance of the evidence in question was outweighed by the potential for unfair prejudice is the sort of argument properly addressed to the District Court. In this case the District Court concluded that the evidence should be admitted, and the Court of Appeals' contrary conclusion was based upon the erroneous, categorical view that testimony about provocative dress and publicly expressed sexual fantasies "had no place in this litigation." 243 U.S. App. D.C., at 328, n. 36, 753 F.2d, at 146, n. 36. While the District Court must carefully weigh the applicable considerations in deciding whether to admit evidence of this kind, there is no per se rule against its admissibility.

III

Although the District Court concluded that respondent had not proved a violation of Title VII, it nevertheless went on to consider the question of the bank's liability. Finding that "the bank was without notice" of Taylor's alleged conduct, and that notice to Taylor was not the equivalent of notice to the bank, the court concluded that the bank therefore could not be held liable for Taylor's alleged actions. The Court of Appeals took the opposite view, holding that an employer is [477 U.S. 57, 70] strictly liable for a hostile environment created by a supervisor's sexual advances, even though the employer neither knew nor reasonably could have known of the alleged misconduct. The court held that a supervisor, whether or not he possesses the authority to hire, fire, or promote, is necessarily an "agent" of his employer for all Title VII purposes, since "even the appearance" of such authority may enable him to impose himself on his subordinates.

The parties and amici suggest several different standards for employer liability. Respondent, not surprisingly, defends the position of the Court of Appeals. Noting that Title VII's definition of "employer" includes any "agent" of the employer, she also argues that "so long as the circumstance is work-related, the supervisor is the employer and the employer is the supervisor." Brief for Respondent 27. Notice to Taylor that the advances were unwelcome, therefore, was notice to the bank.

Petitioner argues that respondent's failure to use its established grievance procedure, or to otherwise put it on notice of the alleged misconduct, insulates petitioner from liability for Taylor's wrongdoing. A contrary rule would be unfair, petitioner argues, since in a hostile environment harassment case the employer often will have no reason to know about, or opportunity to cure, the alleged wrongdoing.

The EEOC, in its brief as amicus curiae, contends that courts formulating employer liability rules should draw from traditional agency principles. Examination of those principles has led the EEOC to the view that where a supervisor exercises the authority actually delegated to him by his employer, by making or threatening to make decisions affecting the employment status of his subordinates, such actions are properly imputed to the employer whose delegation of authority empowered the supervisor to undertake them. Brief for United States and EEOC as

Amici Curiae 22. Thus, the courts have consistently held employers liable for the discriminatory discharges of employees by supervisory personnel, [477 U.S. 57, 71] whether or not the employer knew, should have known, or approved of the supervisor's actions. E.g., Anderson v. Methodist Evangelical Hospital, Inc., 464 F.2d 723, 725 (CA6 1972).

The EEOC suggests that when a sexual harassment claim rests exclusively on a "hostile environment" theory, however, the usual basis for a finding of agency will often disappear. In that case, the EEOC believes, agency principles lead to

"a rule that asks whether a victim of sexual harassment had reasonably available an avenue of complaint regarding such harassment, and, if available and utilized, whether that procedure was reasonably responsive to the employee's complaint. If the employer has an expressed policy against sexual harassment and has implemented a procedure specifically designed to resolve sexual harassment claims, and if the victim does not take advantage of that procedure, the employer should be shielded from liability absent actual knowledge of the sexually hostile environment (obtained, e. g., by the filing of a charge with the EEOC or a comparable state agency). In all other cases, the employer will be liable if it has actual knowledge of the harassment or if, considering all the facts of the case, the victim in question had no reasonably available avenue for making his or her complaint known to appropriate management officials." Brief for United States and EEOC as Amici Curiae 26.

As respondent points out, this suggested rule is in some tension with the EEOC Guidelines, which hold an employer liable for the acts of its agents without regard to notice. 29 CFR 1604.11(c) (1985). The Guidelines do require, however, an "examin[ation of] the circumstances of the particular employment relationship and the job [f]unctions performed by the individual in determining whether an individual acts in either a supervisory or agency capacity." Ibid. [477 U.S. 57, 72]

This debate over the appropriate standard for employer liability has a rather abstract quality about it given the state of the record in this case. We do not know at this stage whether Taylor made any sexual advances toward respondent at all, let alone whether those advances were unwelcome, whether they were sufficiently pervasive to constitute a condition of employment, or whether they were "so pervasive and so long continuing . . . that the employer must have become conscious of [them]," Taylor v. Jones, 653 F.2d 1193, 1197-1199 (CA8 1981) (holding employer liable for racially hostile working environment based on constructive knowledge).

We therefore decline the parties' invitation to issue a definitive rule on employer liability, but we do agree with the EEOC that Congress wanted courts to look to agency principles for guidance in this area. While such common-law principles may not be transferable in all their particulars to Title VII, Congress' decision to define "employer" to include any "agent" of an employer, 42 U.S.C. 2000e(b), surely evinces an intent to place some limits on the acts of employees for which employers under Title VII are to be held responsible. For this reason, we hold that the Court of Appeals erred in concluding that employers are always automatically liable for sexual harassment by their supervisors. See generally Restatement (Second) of Agency 219-237 (1958). For the same reason, absence of notice to an employer does not necessarily insulate that employer from liability. Ibid.

Finally, we reject petitioner's view that the mere existence of a grievance procedure and a policy against discrimination, coupled with respondent's failure to invoke that procedure, must insulate petitioner from liability. While those facts are plainly relevant, the situation before us demonstrates why they are not necessarily dispositive. Petitioner's general nondiscrimination policy did not address sexual harassment in particular, and thus did not alert employees to their employer's [477 U.S. 57, 73] interest in correcting that form of discrimination. App. 25. Moreover, the bank's grievance procedure apparently required an employee to complain first to her supervisor, in this case Taylor. Since Taylor was the alleged perpetrator, it is not altogether surprising that respondent failed to invoke the procedure and report her grievance to him. Petitioner's contention that respondent's failure should insulate it from liability might be substantially stronger if its procedures were better calculated to encourage victims of harassment to come forward.

IV

In sum, we hold that a claim of "hostile environment" sex discrimination is actionable under Title VII, that the District Court's findings were insufficient to dispose of respondent's hostile environment claim, and that the District Court did not err in admitting testimony about respondent's sexually provocative speech and dress. As to employer liability, we conclude that the Court of Appeals was wrong to entirely disregard agency principles and impose absolute liability on employers for the acts of their supervisors, regardless of the circumstances of a particular case.

Accordingly, the judgment of the Court of Appeals reversing the judgment of the District Court is affirmed, and the case is remanded for further proceedings consistent with this opinion.

It is so ordered.

* Like the Court of Appeals, this Court was not provided a complete transcript of the trial. We therefore rely largely on the District Court's opinion for the summary of the relevant testimony.

JUSTICE STEVENS, concurring.

Because I do not see any inconsistency between the two opinions, and because I believe the question of statutory construction that JUSTICE MARSHALL has answered is fairly presented by the record, I join both the Court's opinion and JUSTICE MARSHALL'S opinion. [477 U.S. 57, 74]

JUSTICE MARSHALL, with whom JUSTICE BRENNAN, JUSTICE BLACKMUN, and JUSTICE STEVENS join, concurring in the judgment.

I fully agree with the Court's conclusion that workplace sexual harassment is illegal, and violates Title VII. Part III of the Court's opinion, however, leaves open the circumstances in which an employer is responsible under Title

VII for such conduct. Because I believe that question to be properly before us, I write separately.

The issue the Court declines to resolve is addressed in the EEOC Guidelines on Discrimination Because of Sex, which are entitled to great deference. See Griggs v. Duke Power Co., 401 U.S. 424, 433 -434 (1971) (EEOC Guidelines on Employment Testing Procedures of 1966); see also ante, at 65. The Guidelines explain:

> "Applying general Title VII principles, an employer . . . is responsible for its acts and those of its agents and supervisory employees with respect to sexual harassment regardless of whether the specific acts complained of were authorized or even forbidden by the employer and regardless of whether the employer knew or should have known of their occurrence. The Commission will examine the circumstances of the particular employment relationship and the job [f]unctions performed by the individual in determining whether an individual acts in either a supervisory or agency capacity.

> "With respect to conduct between fellow employees, an employer is responsible for acts of sexual harassment in the workplace where the employer (or its agents or supervisory employees) knows or should have known of the conduct, unless it can show that it took immediate and appropriate corrective action." 29 CFR 1604.11(c),(d) (1985).

The Commission, in issuing the Guidelines, explained that its rule was "in keeping with the general standard of employer [477 U.S. 57, 75] liability with respect to agents and supervisory employees. . . . [T]he Commission and the courts have held for years that an employer is liable if a supervisor or an agent violates the Title VII, regardless of knowledge or any other mitigating factor." 45 Fed. Reg. 74676 (1980). I would adopt the standard set out by the Commission.

An employer can act only through individual supervisors and employees; discrimination is rarely carried out pursuant to a formal vote of a corporation's board of directors. Although an employer may sometimes adopt companywide discriminatory policies violative of Title VII, acts that may constitute Title VII violations are generally effected through the actions of individuals, and often an individual may take such a step even in defiance of company policy. Nonetheless, Title VII remedies, such as reinstatement and backpay, generally run against the employer as an entity. 1 The question thus arises as to the circumstances under which an employer will be held liable under Title VII for the acts of its employees.

The answer supplied by general Title VII law, like that supplied by federal labor law, is that the act of a supervisory employee or agent is imputed to the employer. 2 Thus, for example, when a supervisor discriminatorily fires or refuses to promote a black employee, that act is, without more, considered the act of the employer. The courts do not stop to consider whether the employer otherwise had "notice" of the action, or even whether the supervisor had actual authority to act as he did. E. g., Flowers v. Crouch-Walker Corp., [477 U.S. 57, 76] 552 F.2d 1277, 1282 (CA7 1977); Young v. Southwestern Savings and Loan Assn., 509 F.2d 140 (CA5 1975); Anderson v. Methodist Evangelical Hospital, Inc., 464 F.2d 723 (CA6 1972). Following that approach, every Court of Appeals that has considered the issue has held that sexual harassment by supervisory personnel is automatically imputed to the employer when the harassment results in tangible job detriment to the subordinate employee. See Horn v. Duke Homes, Inc., Div. of Windsor Mobile Homes, 755 F.2d 599, 604-606 (CA7 1985); Craig v. Y & Y Snacks, Inc., 721 F.2d 77, 80-81 (CA3 1983); Katz v. Dole, 709 F.2d 251, 255, n. 6 (CA4 1983); Henson v. Dundee, 682 F.2d 897, 910 (CA11 1982); Miller v. Bank of America, 600 F.2d 211, 213 (CA9 1979).

The brief filed by the Solicitor General on behalf of the United States and the EEOC in this case suggests that a different rule should apply when a supervisor's harassment "merely" results in a discriminatory work environment. The Solicitor General concedes that sexual harassment that affects tangible job benefits is an exercise of authority delegated to the supervisor by the employer, and thus gives rise to employer liability. But, departing from the EEOC Guidelines, he argues that the case of a supervisor merely creating a discriminatory work environment is different because the supervisor "is not exercising, or threatening to exercise, actual or apparent authority to make personnel decisions affecting the victim." Brief for United States and EEOC as Amici Curiae 24. In the latter situation, he concludes, some further notice requirement should therefore be necessary.

The Solicitor General's position is untenable. A supervisor's responsibilities do not begin and end with the power to hire, fire, and discipline employees, or with the power to recommend such actions. Rather, a supervisor is charged with the day-to-day supervision of the work environment and with ensuring a safe, productive workplace. There is no reason why abuse of the latter authority should have different consequences than abuse of the former. In both cases it is the authority [477 U.S. 57, 77] vested in the supervisor by the employer that enables him to commit the wrong: it is precisely because the supervisor is understood to be clothed with the employer's authority that he is able to impose unwelcome sexual conduct on subordinates. There is therefore no justification for a special rule, to be applied only in "hostile environment" cases, that sexual harassment does not create employer liability until the employee suffering the discrimination notifies other supervisors. No such requirement appears in the statute, and no such requirement can coherently be drawn from the law of agency.

Agency principles and the goals of Title VII law make appropriate some limitation on the liability of employers for the acts of supervisors. Where, for example, a supervisor has no authority over an employee, because the two work in wholly different parts of the employer's business, it may be improper to find strict employer liability. See 29 CFR 1604.11(c) (1985). Those considerations, however, do not justify the creation of a special "notice" rule in hostile environment cases.

Further, nothing would be gained by crafting such a rule. In the "pure" hostile environment case, where an employee files an EEOC complaint alleging sexual harassment in the workplace, the employee seeks not money damages but injunctive relief. See Bundy v. Jackson, 205 U.S. App. D.C. 444, 456, n. 12, 641 F.2d 934, 946, n. 12 (1981). Under Title VII, the EEOC must notify an employer of charges made against it within 10 days after receipt of the complaint. 42 U.S.C. 2000e-5(b). If the charges appear to be based on "reasonable cause," the EEOC must attempt to eliminate the offending practice through "informal methods of conference, conciliation, and persuasion." Ibid. An employer whose internal procedures assertedly would have redressed the discrimination can avoid injunctive relief by employing these procedures after receiving notice of the complaint or during the conciliation period. Cf. Brief for United [477 U.S. 57, 78] States and EEOC as Amici Curiae 26. Where a complainant, on the other hand, seeks backpay on the theory that a hostile work environment effected a constructive termination, the existence of an internal complaint procedure may be a factor in determining not the employer's liability but the remedies available against it. Where a complainant without good reason bypassed an internal complaint procedure she knew to be effective, a court may be reluctant to find constructive termination and thus to award reinstatement or backpay.

I therefore reject the Solicitor General's position. I would apply in this case the same rules we apply in all other Title VII cases, and hold that sexual harassment by a supervisor of an employee under his supervision, leading to a discriminatory work environment, should be imputed to the employer for Title VII purposes regardless of whether the employee gave "notice" of the offense.

1. According to the court, how does sexual harassment violate the Civil Rights Act?

EXCERPT FROM *SCOTT BOOTH V. SHERYL RAMSTAD HVASS*, UNITED STATES COURT OF APPEALS FOR THE EIGHTH CIRCUIT, SEPTEMBER 11, 2002

I. BACKGROUND

On October 17, 2000, the plaintiffs-appellants, a group of male Minnesota taxpayers, filed a complaint in the United States District Court for the District of Minnesota, seeking a declaratory judgment that the Minnesota statutory scheme for dispersing state and federal funds to assist battered women and victims of domestic abuse is unconstitutional. The men alleged that the statutory scheme, Minn. Stat. § § 611A.31-375 (2000) (hereinafter "the domestic abuse statutes"), discriminates against men in violation of the Equal Protection Clause of the United States Constitution by facilitating the expenditure of millions of dollars to assist battered women, but offering no money to assist battered males. The appellants also sought an injunction prohibiting the defendants-appellees (various Minnesota State department commissioners) from spending funds under, or promoting the objectives of, the domestic abuse statutes.[1]

Three organizations that provide services and receive funding under the statutes intervened.[2] In January 2001, the appellants moved for summary judgment. The defendants-appellees and intervenors-appellees (collectively "appellees") also moved for summary judgment. The district court held oral argument on the motions. On August 13, 2001, the district court[3] issued an opinion and order denying appellants' motion for summary judgment and granting summary judgment to the appellees. The court concluded that the appellants lacked standing to pursue their claims in federal court.

Appellants timely filed a notice of appeal. On October 9, 2001, appellants filed a statement of issues that included not only the question of appellants' standing, but also the merits of the case. On October 18, the appellees moved this court to limit the issues on appeal to the appellants' standing or, in the alternative, for a prehearing conference. On October 31, an order was entered taking the motion with the case and denying the alternative request for a prehearing conference.

The appellants argue to this court that they have standing as state taxpayers[4] to sue in federal court to prevent the defendants Minnesota state officials from spending public funds under the domestic abuse statutes because the domestic abuse statutes unlawfully discriminate against men based upon their sex.

II. DISCUSSION

We review *de novo* a district court's order granting summary judgment. At the summary judgment stage, the party invoking federal court jurisdiction must set forth by affidavit and other evidence specific facts that, when accepted as true, support a claim of standing. See Campbell v. Minneapolis Pub. Hous. Auth. ex rel. City of Minneapolis, 168 F.3d 1069, 1073 (8th Cir. 1999). We examine whether, after viewing all evidence in a light most favorable to the appellants and drawing all reasonable inferences in their favor, there is a genuine issue as to appellants' standing. See Fed. R. Civ. P. 56(c).

A. PRIOR CASE LAW

In Frothingham v. Mellon, 262 U.S. 447, 487, 43 S. Ct. 597, 67 L. Ed. 1078 (1923), the Supreme Court ruled that a federal taxpayer's interest in United States treasury funds is too small and indeterminable to give that taxpayer standing to sue in federal court. The Court distinguished the municipal taxpayer, who has standing to sue to enjoin the illegal disposition of his or her taxes. Id. at 486 (citing Crampton v. Zabriskie, 101 U.S. 601, 609, 25 L. Ed. 1070 (1880)).

In Doremus v. Board of Educ., 342 U.S. 429, 96 L. Ed. 475, 72 S. Ct. 394 (1952), the Supreme Court determined that a state taxpayer did not have standing in federal court to challenge a state statute that required a Bible reading at the opening of each public school day as a violation of the Establishment Clause. The Court reasoned that the plaintiffs did not allege that the Bible reading "adds any sum whatever to the cost of conducting the school. . . .[Or] that the Bible reading increases any tax they do pay or that as taxpayers they are, will, or possibly can be out of pocket because of it." Id. at 433. The court continued:

> what the Court said of a federal statute as equally true when a state Act is assailed: "The party who invokes the power must be able to show not only that the statute is invalid but that he has sustained or is immediately in danger of sustaining some direct injury as the result of its enforcement, and not merely that he suffers in some indefinite way in common with people generally."

Id. at 434 (quoting Frothingham, 262 U.S. at 488). The taxpayer can meet this test with a "good-faith pocketbook action," which is an injury to the taxpayer's "direct and particular financial interest . . . ." Id. at 434-35.

In 1968, the Court held that a federal taxpayer has standing where: (1) the challenged statute is an exercise of the legislature's taxing and spending powers; and (2) the statute exceeds specific constitutional limitations on those powers. Flast v. Cohen, 392 U.S. 83, 102-03, 106, 20 L. Ed. 2d 947, 88 S. Ct. 1942 (1968). The Court further held that the Establishment Clause is a specific limit on the power of Congress to tax and spend. Id. at 104. While the Court has never declared that the Establishment Clause is the only constitutional provision that satisfies the Flast test for taxpayer standing, it has never found any other constitutional provision that satisfies Flast.

In 1989, we considered whether a taxpayer had standing to challenge a Minnesota statute allowing public high school students to take advanced courses at colleges, some of which were religiously affiliated. See Minnesota Fed'n of Teachers v. Randall, 891 F.2d 1354 (8th Cir. 1989). We determined that the case turned on whether Doremus required a state taxpayer to show that a state's violation of the Establishment Clause increased his or her tax burden, and concluded, in harmony with Flast, that Doremus contained no such requirement. Thus, Randall stands for the proposition that state taxpayers, just like federal taxpayer plaintiffs, "must only show that there has been a disbursement of tax money in potential violation of constitutional guarantees" when bringing Establishment Clause challenges. Randall, 891 F.2d at 1358.

Randall did not completely adopt the Flast test, however. We noted that the Establishment Clause was a specific limit on the taxing and spending power of

Congress, Randall, 891 F.2d at 1356 n.2, but did not address whether state taxpayers must satisfy a requirement that the statute exceed a specific constitutional limit on spending. We specifically mentioned that "the precise scope of Flast [is] uncertain." Randall, 891 F.2d at 1356 n.2.

More recently, in Tarsney v. O'Keefe, 225 F.3d 929 (8th Cir. 2000), we used the Flast test to determine whether a state taxpayer had standing to challenge state funding of abortions for low-income women as a violation of the Free Exercise Clause. In reaching our decision, we reasoned that, whereas expenditure of public money in the aid of religion presents a direct Establishment Clause injury to the taxpayer, no Free Exercise Clause injury arises from a government expenditure until the expenditure directly prevents the taxpayer's free exercise of religion. Id. at 936. Only at that point is the injury direct and taxpayer status irrelevant. Id. We concluded that the Free Exercise Clause was not a constitutional provision that placed a specific limitation on the government's spending.

B. ANALYSIS

The appellants argue that Crampton v. Zabriskie, 101 U.S. 601, 25 L. Ed. 1070 (1880), governs this case. In Crampton, the Supreme Court held that county taxpayers have a direct interest in the application of the county's funds and they may sue for injunctive relief from illegal disposition of those funds. Id. at 609. The Supreme Court reaffirmed this position in Frothingham, 262 U.S. at 486, where it noted that municipal taxpayers have a direct interest in the municipality's application of its moneys, and remedy by injunction is warranted. Appellants argue that under Crampton taxpayers may sue departments of state government (e.g., the departments of Corrections and Public Safety) because those departments, like municipalities and counties, are subdivisions of the state.

We are not convinced by this line of reasoning. In our view, departments of the state are more analogous to the state itself than they are to counties. The taxpayer base for state departments is the same as that of the state. A taxpayer's interest in the funds allocated to a state agency is similar, perhaps identical, to the taxpayer's interest in the general state treasury. Therefore, case law addressing standing for county and municipal taxpayers is inapposite to the instant case.

Appellants also argue that they have standing under Flast itself, as applied in Tarsney. Assuming *arguendo* that the domestic abuse statutes are exercises of state spending power, rather than a regulatory power, appellants' argument requires that we resolve whether the Fourteenth Amendment's Equal Protection Clause is a specific constitutional limit on the spending powers of the Minnesota state government.

Appellants argue that because the Supreme Court's Equal Protection jurisprudence holds that the federal and state governments violate the Equal Protection Clause when they fund discriminatory institutions, the Equal Protection Clause can be a limitation on the taxing and spending powers of government. Appellants cite a number of Supreme Court cases to support this argument. E.g. Mississippi Univ. for Women v. Hogan 458 U.S. 718, 73 L. Ed. 2d 1090, 102 S. Ct. 3331 (1982) (holding the Equal Protection Clause barred sex discrimination in admissions to state supported nursing school); Frontiero v. Richardson

411 U.S. 677, 36 L. Ed. 2d 583, 93 S. Ct. 1764 (1973) (holding that the Equal Protection Clause barred sex discrimination in public spending for benefits to military personnel). The cases cited by the appellants are distinguishable from the instant case. Standing was not an issue in any of them; the plaintiffs all alleged direct injuries.

Appellants continue their argument by analogy, contending that because public schools receive tax dollars, a taxpayer would have standing to challenge state funding of a school that is racially or sexually discriminatory in its admissions. Under this theory, appellants believe they have shown that the Equal Protection Clause acts as a specific limit on governmental spending. Finally, under Flast, the appellants argue that they have taxpayer standing to challenge the alleged equal protection violation perpetrated by Minnesota under the domestic abuse statutes.

Our line of precedent leads us to the opposite conclusion. Under Tarsney, in order to determine whether the Equal Protection Clause is a specific limitation on the taxing and spending powers of state government, we consider whether the expenditure of public funds in a discriminatory manner violates the Equal Protection Clause. A taxpayer whose tax money is used in a discriminatory manner suffers no injury under the Equal Protection Clause unless and until an expenditure facilitates discrimination against him or her. At that point, taxpayer status is irrelevant to standing. In this case, the appellants do not have taxpayer standing to challenge state expenditures to benefit battered women under the Equal Protection Clause.

III. CONCLUSION

The appellants lack taxpayer standing to bring suit in federal court. We affirm the district court's grant of summary judgment of dismissal.

1. According to the plaintiffs, how is funding for women's shelters unconstitutional?

2. On what grounds does the court deny their appeal? Do you agree? Why or why not?

"APPEALS COURT SLASHES AWARD AGAINST ASARCO IN SEXUAL HARASSMENT CASE" BY BRANDON BROWN, FROM *CRONKITE NEWS*, OCTOBER 24, 2013

WASHINGTON – A federal appeals court Thursday slashed the damages that mining company ASARCO had been ordered to pay a former employee who successfully sued the company for sexual harassment at an Arizona mine. A divided three-judge panel of the 9th U.S. Circuit Court of Appeals said the $300,000 in punitive damages awarded to Angela Aguilar was excessive in comparison to the $1 in nominal damages a jury awarded her.

While the court said ASARCO's conduct in Aguilar's case was "highly reprehensible" and merited "the imposition of a very large punitive award," it said $300,000 was out of line. It sent the case back to district court, where it said Aguilar could accept a lower award of $125,000 or the case could go back to trial.

"It would have been nice to keep the whole thing," Aguilar's attorney, Sandy Forbes, said, "but we are pleased."

Calls to ASARCO and its attorneys were not immediately returned Thursday.

Aguilar began working in 2005 at ASARCO's Mission Mine complex in Sahuarita, where she said her supervisor, Wayne Johnson, continuously asked her out and would press up against her when she asked for help, according to the court.

Because there was no women's restroom at the filter plant where she worked, Aguilar had to use a portable toilet that was soon "vandalized with pornographic graffiti directed at her."

Complaints to company officials "initially fell on deaf ears," the court said, and Aguilar asked for and got a transfer to another unit.

In June 2006, she transferred to the main mill building, where the court said she reported to Julio Esquivel. But court documents said Esquivel would yell at Aguilar and threaten to have her fired, telling her before she even started working with him, "Your ass is mine."

After taking leave in September 2006, Aguilar returned to work briefly in November before quitting after four days.

Arizona sued ASARCO in 2008 under the state's civil rights act, and Aguilar later filed her own harassment suit against the company.

After an eight-day trial in U.S. District Court, a jury found ASARCO liable for the sexual harassment claims and awarded Aguilar $868,750 in punitive damages, $1 in nominal damages and no compensatory damages.

The district court later lowered the punitive damages to $300,000, the maximum allowable under Title VII, and said that amount was not constitutionally excessive.

But the appeals court Thursday cited Supreme Court rulings that punitive damages "must bear a reasonable relationship to compensatory damages," and that was not the case here.

The appeals court said it was not bound by the Supreme Court's suggestion that there not be more than a single-digit ratio between compensatory and punitive damages, but it said "a 300,000-to-1 ratio raises our 'judicial eyebrow(s).'"

It settled on $125,000, citing the next-highest ratio it could find in another circuit. That amount brought a "reasonable relationship" between the award amounts, but was still "proportional to the reprehensibility of ASARCO's conduct."

In a partial dissent, Judge Andrew D. Hurwitz said he agreed with most of the majority opinion but that he would have left the award at $300,000.

Forbes said she had not discussed next steps in the case with Aguilar yet. Calls to the Attorney General's Office for comment were not immediately returned.

1. On what grounds did the court decide to limit Aguilar's settlement?

2. What do cases like Aguilar's tell us about sexual harassment lawsuits?

CHAPTER 4

WHAT ADVOCACY ORGANIZATIONS SAY

Advocacy organizations are on the forefront of the fight against sexual harassment and gender violence all over the world. Groups like RAINN, Advocates Against Domestic Violence (AADV), and the National Coalition Against Domestic Violence (NCADV) are leading the way in empowering victims, gathering research, and pushing for legislation that better addresses the needs of men and women who have been traumatized. International groups like United Nations Women, End Violence Against Women International (EVAWI), and CARE work with governments around the globe to better address the root causes of gender-based violence and discrimination, while also providing resources to those in need. These groups are often in direct contact with those impacted by gender violence and sexual harassment, making their voices all the more crucial as we learn about these important issues. They bring the on-the-ground perspective that can often be lost as we discuss complex problems and help us understand how legislation impacts people's lives.

EXCERPT FROM THE "INTERNATIONAL GUIDE TO ADDRESSING GENDER-BASED VIOLENCE THROUGH SPORT" BY SARA MURRAY, FROM WOMEN WIN

THE IMPACT

When a woman experiences gender-based violence, the physical and emotional impact is lasting and seeps into every sphere of a woman's life. Sexual abuse and rape survivors exhibit a variety of trauma-induced symptoms including sleep and eating disturbances, depression, feelings of humiliation, anger and self blame, fear of sex, and an inability to concentrate.[7]

Beyond the emotional trauma, GBV can result in physical injuries, contraction of sexual transmitted infections, including HIV, interruptions to sexual health and reproductive abilities, unwanted pregnancies and even death.

Due to the sensitivity of the subject, violence against women is universally under-reported.[8] Compounding the personal devastation is the reality that this type of violence is often shrouded in secrecy, prohibiting women from accessing the legal and medical resources they need to cope. Survivors of GBV often feel shame, an instinct to protect the family unit and conflicting allegiances, which makes discussing the problem difficult. It is not uncommon for women to be blamed for their own rape and to be considered as bringing dishonour to their families. Beyond this reluctance, in many regions of the world, reporting violence can lead to more violence for women, at

the hands of police, officials and perpetrators. The fear of
retribution further inhibits women in seeking needed legal
help, medical services and counselling, thereby continuing
a cycle of devastation. Honour killings are also quite
common. In some countries family honour is dependent on
the behaviour of women.

Programme Partner MIFUMI (Uganda)

While working with women and girls suffering
from GBV, it is not unusual for women to deny or
attempt to minimise the severity of their injury.
For example, girls/women saying "I knocked myself
against a wall in the dark" when, in actuality,
she was beaten. MIFUMI has taken a key role in
sensitising the community through the radio. They
stress the need to be open about violence because
such candidness can reduce the stigma. In addition,
the "Sure Start" project run by MIFUMI trains the
teachers, medical personnel and other district
leaders such as probation officers to identify and
address problems of GBV even when the victim is
hiding the reality. Success has also been achieved
in having a referral network through the Tororo
district Child Actors Network and the MIFUMI-
specific advice centres for women and girls.

THE COST

Consider the negative impact GBV has on the individual and her family, and multiply it by a billion. The result is catastrophic across global and regional sectors and a major inhibitor to global development. By sapping women's energy, undermining their confidence, and compromising their health, gender-based violence deprives society of women's full participation. As the U.N. Women (formerly UNIFEM) observed, "Women cannot lend their labour or creative ideas fully if they are burdened with the physical and psychological scars of abuse."[9]

PUBLIC HEALTH AND ECONOMICS

Gender-based violence poses significant costs for the economies of developing countries and the individual, including lower worker productivity and incomes, lower rates of accumulation of human and social capital, and the generation of other forms of violence both now and in the future. GBV also puts an undue burden on public health. Women who experience GBV are likely to have an increased need for health services dealing with physical and emotional treatment.[10] They are also more inclined to experience maternal mortality, unwanted pregnancies and more likely to contract sexually transmitted diseases, including HIV/AIDS. Through its impact on future sexual and drug using behaviour, sexual abuse in childhood also appears to[11] increase an individual's risk of contracting STDs and HIV in adulthood.[12]

The economic impact of GBV can be understood both in terms of money spent on services, as well as a loss in productivity by women and their family members who have been impacted. Money spent on medical, legal and social services is money not being spent elsewhere in national economies – including food and education – critical components to alleviation of poverty. Compromises to individual economic contributions due to GBV often come in the form of job loss, lost productivity of the abuser due to incarceration, and loss of tax revenues due to death and incarceration.

For survivors, the physical injury and psychological trauma has long-term consequences on education. Acute depression, stigma and isolation often have a negative impact on educational performance or lead to girls dropping out of school all together. In cases of community and state violence, the threat posed by violence in public space can make parents unwilling to allow girls to make the journey to school.

ROOTS OF POWER, GENDER, AND VIOLENCE

According to the U.N. Declaration on the Elimination of Violence Against Women (1993), "violence against women is a manifestation of historically unequal power relations between men and women, which has led to domination over and discrimination against women by men and to the prevention of the full advancement of women, and that violence against women is one of the crucial social mechanisms by which women are forced into a subordinate position compared with men."[14]

In most places, men possess more economic, political, domestic, and overall decision making power than women. Research has shown that violence is instrumental in maintaining control of that power. More than 90 percent of "systematic, persistent, and injurious" violence is perpetrated by men.[15]

The deep interplay of gender, power and violence is far too complex to adequately unpack in this guide. However, understanding, on a basic level, the fact that violence follows power in a social context, is a building block to being able to adequately address it from a personal and programmatic perspective. It is important to recognise that men and boys also experience violence, the impact of which can be devastating to individuals and groups. However, because of the uneven impact of gender-based violence on women and girls and the nature of this guide, our focus will be on females.

TERMS

In order to have a conversation about any issue, all parties must agree on a common language. Below is a breakdown of words used throughout this guide. When participating in conversation on this platform, this will become our collective baseline. Whenever possible, these definitions have been extracted from United Nations sources, to ensure universal applicability and legal agreement. […]

Abuse: is the systematic pattern of behaviours in a relationship that are used to gain and/or maintain control and power over another.[16]

Empowerment: is the process of people taking control over their lives, pursuing their own goals, living according to their own values, developing self-reliance, and being able to make choices, transform those choices into actions, and influence – both individually and collectively – the decisions that affect their lives.[17]

Femicide: is on the extreme end of a continuum of anti-female terror that includes a wide variety of verbal and physical abuse, such as rape, torture, sexual slavery (particularly in prostitution), incestuous and extra-familial child sexual abuse, physical and emotional battery, sexual harassment (on the phone, in the streets, at the office, and in the classroom), genital mutilation, psycho-surgery and denial of food to women in some cultures. Whenever these forms of terrorism result in death, they become femicides.[18]

Gender: refers to the social attributes and opportunities associated with being male and female and the relation-ships between women and men and girls and boys, as well as the relations between women and those between men. These attributes, opportunities and relationships are socially constructed and are learned through socialization processes. They are context/time-specific and change-able. Gender determines what is expected, allowed and valued in a woman or a man in a given context.[19]

Gender Discrimination: is any distinction, exclusion or restriction made on the basis of sex which has the effect or purpose of impairing or nullifying the recognition, enjoyment or exercise by either men women, irrespec-tive of their marital status, on a basis of equality of men and women, of human rights and fundamental freedoms in the political, economic, social, cultural, civil or any other field.[20]

Gender Equality: indicates that women and men have equal conditions for realizing their full human rights and for contributing to, and benefiting from, economic, social, cultural and political development. Gender equality is therefore the equal valuing by society of the similarities and the differences of men and women, and the roles they play. It is based on women and men being full partners in their home, their community and their society. Gender equality starts with equal valuing of girls and boys.[21]

Gender Roles: are a set of social and behavioural norms that are considered to be socially appropriate for individuals of a specific sex in the context of a specific culture, which differ widely between cultures and over time.[22]

Gender-based Violence: is any act that results in, or is likely to result in, physical, sexual or psychological harm or suffering to women, including threats of such acts, coercion or arbitrary deprivations of liberty, whether occurring in public or in private life. This encompasses, but is not limited to, acts of physical, sexual, and psychological violence in the family, community, or perpetrated or condoned by the State, wherever it occurs. These acts include: spousal battery; sexual abuse, including of female children; dowry-related violence; rape, including marital rape; female genital mutilation/cutting and other traditional practices harmful to women; non-spousal violence; sexual violence related to exploitation; sexual harassment and intimidation at work, in school and elsewhere; trafficking in women; and forced prostitution. In 1995, the U.N. expanded the definition to include: violations of the rights of women in situations of armed conflict, including systematic rape, sexual slavery and forced pregnancy; forced sterilization, forced abortion, coerced or forced use of contraceptives; prenatal sex selection and female infanticide. It further recognised the particular vulnerabilities of women belonging to minorities: the elderly and the displaced; indigenous, refugee and migrant communities; women living in impoverished rural or remote areas, or in detention.

Human Rights: are basic rights and freedoms that all people are entitled to regardless of nationality, sex, national or ethnic origin, race, religion, language, or other status. These entitlements include civil and political rights, such as the right to life, liberty and freedom of expression; and social, cultural and economic rights including the right to participate in culture, the right to food, the right to work, play and receive an education. Human rights are protected and upheld by international and national laws and treaties.[23]

Infanticide: is the putting to death of the newborn with the consent of the parent, family or community.[24]

PEP Test: is an acronym for post exposure prophylaxis, a course of antiretroviral drugs which is thought to reduce the risk of infection after events with high risk of exposure to HIV, including voluntary vaginal or anal intercourse and rape. PEP test is most effective if administered within an hour of infection, but no longer than 72 hours.[25]

Perpetrator: is a person who commits or knowingly allows maltreatment or a crime against another person or group.

Poverty: is the total absence of opportunities, accompanied by high levels of undernourishment, hunger, illiteracy, lack of education, physical and mental ailments, emotional and social instability, unhappiness, sorrow and hopelessness for the future. Poverty is also characterized by a chronic shortage of economic, social and political participation, relegating individuals to exclusion as social beings, preventing access to the benefits of economic and social development and thereby limiting their cultural development.[26]

Power: is possession of control, authority or influence over others; the ability to act or produce an effect; mental or moral efficacy; political control or influence.[27]

Rape: is any forced or coerced genital contact or sexual penetration.

Sexual Harassment: such unwelcome sexually determined behaviour as physical contact and advances, sexually coloured remarks, showing pornography and sexual demands, whether by words or actions. Such conduct can be humiliating and may constitute a health and safety problem; it is discriminatory when the woman has reasonable ground to believe that her objection would disadvantage her in connection with her employment, including recruitment or promotion, or when it creates a hostile working environment.[28]

Stereotype[s]: are beliefs held about characteristics, traits, and activity-domains that are deemed appropriate for men and women.[29]

Survivor: is one who lives through affliction, violence, harassment or abuse.

Systematic Rape: is a brutal tactic used in times of war to terrorize women by sexually assaulting them. It has also been used as a means to perform ethnic cleansing by degrading and demoralizing the persecuted ethnic group. According to international law, systematic rape has been declared a crime against humanity as well as a war crime. It is also one of the criteria used to identify genocide.[30]

Violence: is the intentional use of physical force or power, threatened or actual, against oneself, another person, or against a group or community that either results in or has a high likelihood of resulting in injury, death, psychological harm, underdevelopment, or deprivation.[31]

1. According to the author, what are the roots of gender violence?

2. According to the author, what are some of the costs of gender violence?

"CHANGING THE CULTURE OF DOMESTIC VIOLENCE ONE QUILT SQUARE AT A TIME" BY VICTORIA LAW, FROM *WAGING NONVIOLENCE*, JANUARY 26, 2015

Two hundred years ago, quilts were an integral part of the Underground Railroad. Abolitionists sewed patterns into the squares of their quilts. They then hung the quilts in their yards, ostensibly to air them out. Runaway slaves could use the squares to identify friendly people, possible guides, preparations and directions towards freedom.

This Tuesday, January 27, quilt squares will once again serve as a beacon towards freedom. In Jacksonville, Fla., the lawn outside the Duval County Courthouse will be blanketed with quilt squares. The reason: to bring attention to and protest the continued prosecution of Marissa Alexander, a black woman, mother of three and domestic violence survivor. Collected by the Monument Quilt, an ongoing project that crowd-sources stories of domestic and sexual violence, each of the 350 four-foot by four-foot squares contains a message about domestic violence or sexual assault. By sharing stories of domestic and sexual violence, the quilt also transforms the prosecution's narrative that Alexander was the aggressor and, instead, examines her case in the context of a culture where domestic violence and sexual assault are pervasive and often condoned.

In 2010, nine days after giving birth to a premature baby girl, Alexander was attacked by her estranged husband Rico Grey. It was not the first time he assaulted her, but this time, after unsuccessfully trying to escape, Alexander tried to ward him off by firing a warning shot. Her husband stopped, left the house and called the police. Although no one had been hurt, Alexander was arrested and charged with aggravated assault with a deadly weapon.

Alexander's trial highlights how the experiences of domestic violence survivors are disbelieved and dismissed by the legal system. Before the trial, Grey admitted, as part of a 66-page deposition, that he had not only abused Alexander during their relationship, but had also been abusive to the other four women with whom he had children. Nonetheless, the district attorney continued with her prosecution.

During her trial, evidence of Grey's continued violence towards Alexander was presented, including testimony by family members. Nonetheless, the judge instructed the jury to consider self-defense only if Alexander had proven, beyond a reasonable doubt, that her husband was committing aggravated battery when she fired. His instructions shifted the burden of proof from the prosecutor onto Alexander. The jury deliberated for only 12 minutes before convicting her. The prosecutor then chose to add Florida's 10-20-Life sentencing enhancement, which requires a 20-year mandatory sentence if a firearm is discharged.

The prosecution and incarceration of domestic violence survivors is not uncommon. As I've mentioned in earlier columns, domestic violence is widespread, both in and out of prison. The U.S. Department of Justice found that more than half of the women in local jails and state prisons have experienced past physical and sexual violence from their loved ones. But when abuse survivors face the court system, they have to overcome narratives that deny their experiences of violence or blame them for it. No one knows how often they succeed since there are no nationwide statistics on how many women are in prison for abuse-related convictions.

Unlike many other survivors in the criminal punishment system, Alexander's case captured national attention. Her sentencing coincided with George Zimmerman's shooting of Trayvon Martin, thus eliciting comparisons in the use of Florida's Stand Your Ground law, under which a person who has a reasonable fear of death or harm is allowed to threaten or use force that may harm, or even kill, their presumed assailant. A pretrial judge denied Alexander's attempt to argue Stand Your Ground; Zimmerman, on the other hand, was allowed to utilize the statute as his defense and was ultimately acquitted. That Angela Corey prosecuted both cases provoked further attention — and outrage.

People across the country, many of whom are survivors of domestic violence and anti-violence activists, mobilized to help overturn her conviction, forming the Free Marissa Now campaign to highlight the injustice of the legal system's re-victimization of a survivor of domestic violence. They organized teach-ins and fundraisers, both in their respective cities and towns as well as online. The protracted outreach worked. Media picked up on the difference in treatment between Zimmerman's and Alexander's attempts to argue Stand Your Ground, with guests on talk shows and bloggers bringing Alexander's name into the nationwide discussions about George Zimmerman, Trayvon Martin and the concept of self-defense.

In September 2013, an appeals court overturned her conviction, determining that the judge's instructions were flawed, and ordered that she receive a new trial. Alexander was held in prison for two more months before being released on a $200,009 bond. In the meantime, the Free Marissa Now campaign continued to draw attention to her continued prosecution. Poet Nikky Finney wrote a poem called "Flare," both about Alexander's specific case as well as the history of the devaluing of black women's lives. Finney and other supporters invited various people (including me) to film themselves reading the poem, then spread the videos through social media to continue drawing attention to her case.

They continued to organize fundraisers in various cities as well as online to pay for Alexander's bond payment and ankle monitor — not to mention the legal fees for her upcoming trial. Artists, including Molly Crabapple, Dignidad Rebelde and Bianca Diaz, created and donated art that was reproduced on buttons and t-shirts. Between November 2013 and March 2014, supporters raised more than $63,000.

But the outpouring of public support, which included hundreds of letters urging her to drop the case, did not sway Florida prosecutor Angela Corey, who vowed to seek a 60-year sentence for Alexander. On Nov. 24, Alexander accepted a plea deal which includes time served for the 1,030 days she spent behind bars, an additional 65 days in jail and two years of house arrest while wearing an ankle monitor. During those two years, she will be responsible for the $105 weekly cost of her ankle monitor, a total of $10,920. Alexander was immediately taken to the Duval County Jail to await her Jan. 27 sentencing hearing.

Supporters continue to mobilize around her case. On Jan. 17, 10 days before Alexander's sentencing date, supporters kicked off a campaign called 10 Days to Black Freedom, planning to raise $10,000 to cover the $10,920 of the ankle monitor. Within three days, they had already exceeded their goal, which will not only enable Alexander to pay for the ankle monitor, but also cover other expenses she may incur while unable to work — or even leave her house without prior permission — for the next two years.

Supporters are also planning to converge in Jacksonville in a demonstration of support on the day of Alexander's sentencing. Nearly a dozen have formed the East Bay Caravan, traveling from Oakland to Jacksonville to attend the sentencing. Their two-week journey includes stops in approximately 15 cities where they held teach-ins, dropped banners, distributed fliers and engaged with local activists. Organizers from the Baltimore-based Monument Quilt project will also be driving south, bringing with them a quilt of stories measuring 100 by 150 feet.

Rebecca Nagle is an organizer with the Monument Quilt, which uses quilting to raise awareness and create a public space to heal. "We're changing the culture from one of public shaming of survivors to one of public support for survivors," she said. Noting that sympathetic coverage of domestic violence survivors often excludes those who are not young, white and heterosexual, Nagle points out that a quilt "can tell many different stories at once. We're creating a highly public narrative that encompasses these different stories."

The Monument Quilt connected with the Free Marissa Now campaign while on tour this past summer. Originally, organizers planned to bring the quilt to Jacksonville for the first day of Alexander's trial. When Alexander accepted a plea bargain, they shifted their focus to her sentencing date.

"The quilt puts her prosecution and story in the context of domestic violence, which happens to a lot of women," stated Nagle. "So does the prosecution of many domestic violence survivors."

Approximately 50 people responded to the call to create quilt squares specifically supporting Alexander. Some squares came from organizations like the Inheritance Quilt, a domestic violence awareness project; the Black Student Alliance at Yale University; and Power Inside, an advocacy group working with incarcerated women in Maryland. Individuals also created squares.

Some state "Free Marissa Now" or ask, "How can you prosecute people for surviving?" Others are created by people who have lost loved ones to domestic violence-related murders. "My father murdered my mother in front of me and my brother," stated one.

Nagle remembered a November quilt-making workshop in which a woman brought her six-year-old grandson. "She had talked with him beforehand about the intergenerational trauma of violence," she recalled. At the workshop, the boy created a square that promised, "I vow to be a safe man."

There is the possibility that, on Jan. 27, the judge will sentence Alexander not to house arrest, but to more time in prison. "It's important for people to still support her," Nagle said. And, no matter what the outcome, she noted, "The problem of women being prosecuted for self-defense, particularly women of color who are disproportionately impacted by the legal system, doesn't stop with Marissa Alexander."

1. How can crafting help combat gender violence?

"THE VIOLENCE AGAINST WOMEN REAUTHORIZATION ACT OF 2013 SUMMARY OF SUBSTANTIVE CHANGES" BY ROBERT LAKE, FROM MICHIGAN POVERTY LAW PROGRAM, AUGUST 12, 2013

I. INTRODUCTION

The Violence Against Women Act (VAWA)[1] – first passed in 1994 and previously reauthorized in 2000 and 2005 – is comprehensive legislation that specifically seeks to protect victims of domestic violence, dating violence, sexual assault, and stalking, and attempts to remedy laws and practices that have historically subjected women[2] to these crimes, through federal grant programs, research, and criminal penalties. After languishing in Congressional gridlock for over a year, the 2013 reauthorization[3] passed the Senate on February 12, 2013 (78-22) and the House of Representatives on February 28, 2013 (286-138). President Obama signed the act into law on March 7, 2013. VAWA 2013 expands and improves upon earlier protections and programs in a number of substantive ways.

A. STATISTICS

Studies show that domestic violence, dating violence, sexual assault, and stalking affect millions of Americans each year. "More than one-third of women in the United States (35.6% or approximately 42.4 million) have experienced rape, physical violence, and/or stalking by an intimate partner at some point in their lifetime."[4] One in 3 women fall victim to severe physical violence by an intimate partner.[5] In 2010 alone, 1,095 women were killed by their current [or] former husbands and boyfriends.[6]

Violence is prevalent among dating youth[7] as well. A government study reported 9.3% of high school-aged female subjects had been hit, slapped, or physically hurt in the year preceding the survey, and roughly 335,000 females experience severe dating violence each year.[8]

Data concerning sexual assault is similarly alarming. Nearly 1 in 5 (18.3%) women have been raped,[9] and 1 in 10 will be raped by their intimate partner.[10] 51.1% of victims are raped by an intimate partner and 40.8% by an acquaintance.[11] Further, nearly 1 in 2 women (44.6%) have been sexually assaulted in some way *other than* rape in their lifetime.[12]

Last, approximately 1 in 6 women (16.2 percent) in the United States have been a victim of stalking.[13]

B. EFFECTIVENESS

It is difficult to determine the total number of people served across all VAWA-related programs, but the Office on Violence Against Women (OVW) — which administers most of the grant programs authorized under VAWA — prepared a report for Congress detailing its services from July 1, 2009 to June 30, 2011, broken in 6-month "reporting periods." Thirteen OVW grantees reported "serving an average of 125,726 victims/survivors[14] during each 6-month reporting period between July 1, 2009 and June 30, 2011; this represents more than 97 percent of all victims/survivors who requested services."[15] During this same reporting period, "1,191 VAWA grantees trained 661,263 professionals, including police officers, victim advocates, health care professionals, and attorneys…"[16]

The original passage of VAWA in 1994, and the subsequent implementation of its programs, is positively correlated with a decrease in violence against women. Specifically, a 2012 Bureau of Justice Statistics study reports that "[f]rom 1994 to 2010, the overall rate of intimate partner violence in the United States declined by 64%, from 9.8 victimizations per 1,000 persons age 12 or older to 3.6 per 1,000."[17] That said, VAWA critics point out that "this decrease happened at the same time violent crime as a whole fell dramatically [four-fold] nationwide, making it hard to know whether a drop in domestic violence might have happened without the policies adopted under VAWA."[18] VAWA proponents further point to economic gains under the act; a 2002 study asserts that in its first six years, VAWA saved the country $12.6 billion in "net averted social costs."[19] A 2009 study of the Kentucky justice system also showed savings to taxpayers.[20]

II. SUBSTANTIVE CHANGE IN VAWA 2013

Upon passage of VAWA 2013 by Congress, Attorney General Eric Holder proclaimed the act to be, "a landmark law that has transformed the way we respond to domestic and sexual violence. This reauthorization includes crucial new provisions to improve our ability to bring hope and healing to the victims of these crimes, expand access to justice, and strengthen the prosecutorial and enforcement tools available to hold perpetrators accountable."[21] The new law seeks to expand the federal protections and available resources of the original act, and to ensure that previously unrepresented classes of victim now too can get the help they need, while being mindful of the current economic climate. VAWA 2013 addresses these goals in a number of ways:

1. Tightens funding and grants;

2. Improves protection of subsidized housing residents;

3. Improves protection of immigrants;

4. Expands the federal stalking statute;

5. Intensifies focus on sexual assault;

6. Extends protection to lesbian, gay, bisexual, and transgender survivors;

7. Informs and empowers college students; and

8. Extends protection and justice to Native Americans

A. TIGHTENS FUNDING AND GRANTS:

The Congressional Budget Office estimates that Congress will authorize $3.2 billion for fiscal years 2013-2018 for VAWA programs,[22] a 17% cut from the 2005 reauthorization.[23] In a further effort to save money, VAWA 2013 consolidates 13 programs into 4, thereby reducing administrative and service overlap, and adds new accountability measures that "include strict new audit requirements, enforcement mechanisms for grantees that fail to fix problems found in the audits, restrictions on grantees' executive compensation and investments and their administrative costs."[24]

The vast majority of VAWA funds are distributed in the form of grants by the OVW. "As of October 2012, VAWA funds 18 discretionary grant programs, the comprehensive technical assistance provider initiative (Technical Assistance Program), and 3 formula grant programs — the STOP Program, the Sexual Assault Services (SASP) Formula Grant Program, and the Grants to State Sexual

Assault and Domestic Violence Coalitions Program (State Coalitions Program). In addition, VAWA funds several special initiatives to enhance victim safety and autonomy, increase the availability of victim services, and enhance offender accountability."[25]

B. IMPROVES PROTECTION OF SUBSIDIZED HOUSING RESIDENTS:

The 2005 reauthorization introduced measures to help prevent discrimination against domestic violence survivors living in, or attempting to enter, public housing. VAWA 2013 expands the scope of this coverage to all federally funded housing, adds protection to sexual assault victims, and provides for emergency housing transfers.

Studies have shown that "domestic violence is a primary cause of homelessness; that 92% of homeless women have experienced severe physical or sexual abuse at some point in their lives; that victims of violence have experienced discrimination by landlords; and that victims of domestic violence often return to abusive partners because they cannot find long-term housing."[26] VAWA 2005 recognized a need to address these intersections of violence and housing, and introduced measures to help prevent discrimination against domestic violence survivors living in, or attempting to enter, subsidized housing.

VAWA 2013 continues and expands upon many of the protections provided by VAWA 2005. Specifically, VAWA 2013 prohibits public housing authorities (PHAs), programs, owners, and managers from discriminating against applicants or tenants who are survivors of domestic violence, dating violence, sexual assault, and stalking. Further, incidents of abuse may not be considered good cause for terminating the lease or public assistance, unless the other tenants or employees are in actual or imminent danger.

Significant changes are as follows:

Eligible Housing: VAWA 2013 expands the list of covered housing programs, which now includes additional HUD programs, as well as programs administered by the Department of Agriculture and Department of Treasury:

- Department of Housing and Urban Development (HUD)
- Public housing
- Section 8 project-based housing
- Section 8 vouched-based housing
- Section 202 elderly housing
- Section 811 disabled housing
- Section 236 multifamily rental housing*
- HOME*
- Section 221(d)(3) Below Market Interest Rate*
- Housing Opportunities for People with Aids*
- McKinney-Vento Act programs*
- Department of Agriculture
- Rural Development multifamily housing*
- Department of Treasury
- Low-Income Housing Tax Credit*

* Program newly included for coverage under VAWA 2013

Protected Parties: VAWA 2013 added survivors of sexual assault to those covered by housing protections. Thus, under VAWA 2013, these parties include anyone living in or applying for admission to a covered housing program who is a victim of domestic violence, dating violence, sexual assault, or stalking, or is an "affiliated individual" of the victim, such as a spouse, brother, child, or tenant. The household member need *not* be related to the victim by blood or marriage to receive protection.

Emergency Unit Transfers: Federal agencies must develop and adopt a plan that provides the means for a victim tenant to move to another covered housing unit if the tenant requests the transfer, and reasonably believes that harm is imminent or, in cases of sexual assault, if the assault occurred 90 days before the request.

Delivery of Notification: VAWA 2013 mandates that HUD must inform applicants and tenants of their rights in an approved and written "HUD notice," which must be available in multiple languages.

Lease Bifurcation: If a tenant or lawful occupant commits a violent act against another tenant or lawful occupant, the PHA, owner, or manager may bifurcate the lease and evict the perpetrator, while allowing the survivor to remain in the unit. VAWA 2013 grants the survivor some additional protection. Namely, any remaining tenant has the opportunity to establish eligibility to remain in the unit and, if unable to do so, must be given reasonable time to find new housing.

Victim Status Certification: VAWA 2013 revises the process by which PHAs, owners, and managers can request written certification that an applicant or tenant is a victim of domestic violence, dating violence, sexual assault, or stalking. PHAs, owners, and managers are now permitted, but not required, to request certification on a federal agency-approved form. Further, the victim may now also provide a statement signed by a mental health professional or an administrative record to document the abuse. The applicant has 14 business days to respond to the request; otherwise, the PHA, owner, or manager may deny admission or begin the eviction process.

Confidentiality: A PHA, owner, or manager must keep a victim's certification information confidential and may not store it on a shared database or disclose it to another individual or organization, except by permission or when required by law.

C. IMPROVES PROTECTION OF IMMIGRANTS:

VAWA 2013 maintains key protections, while strengthening and improving specific provisions, such as those concerning self-petitioners, U visa holders, and the International Marriage Broker Regulation Act.

Studies examining domestic violence in immigrant populations are limited, but data does suggest that immigrant or refugee women are at special risk for domestic violence, with conditions such as language barriers, immigration status, traditional values, lack of education, and economic dependence increasing their vulnerability.[27] In these situations, an abusive lawful permanent resident may use immigration requirements to maintain control over an abused immigrant spouse.

VAWA addressed these concerns in 1994, and revisited the issue in 2000 and 2005. These laws allowed a battered non-citizen spouse and children to gain legal immigration status without the involvement of the abusive lawful citizen spouse. In this situation, the abused spouse applicant is the principle, and the children are derivatives. The 2013 reauthorization continues to refine and expand this idea in a variety of ways. First, stalking is now a crime covered by the U visa. Next, in cases of abusive marriages shown to be invalid by bigamy, the battered immigrant spouse may be eligible for a hardship waiver. However, this exception applies only in cases of battery or extreme cruelty and not for things like divorce or death. Third, surviving children of VAWA self-petitioners may still be eligible for some benefits while the application is pending or approved. Additionally, VAWA and U visa petitioners, as well as other "qualified alien" battered immigrants, may not be barred from becoming lawful permanent residents on the grounds of past utilization of public assistance. Last, VAWA 2013 protects the status of child derivative U visa applicant while his/her principal's application is under consideration. Specifically, if the derivative U visa applicant was under 21 when the principal filed his/her application, then the derivative will continue to be classified as a child even if he/she turns 21 while the principal's application is pending. Further, if a *principal* applicant is under 21 at the time of filing, then he/she will remain classified as a child applicant.

VAWA 2013 also strengthens the International Marriage Broker Regulation Act of 2005 (IMBRA), which seeks to regulate so-called "mail-order bride" agencies. The IMBRA requires [that] IMBs perform background checks on their US clients and disclose this information to their foreign clients. Further, the IMBRA placed a cap on the number of fiancé visa petitions an individual may file over a given period.

D. EXPANDS THE FEDERAL STALKING STATUTE

VAWA 2013 expands the scope of § 2261A, the federal stalking statute, in two main ways: (1) stalking no longer requires actual harm; and (2) it is now easier to trigger the statute in cyberstalking cases. The following allows for comparison between the old and new statutes:

§ 2261A. Stalking
18 U.S.C.A. § 2261A (2006)
Whoever--
(1) travels in interstate or foreign commerce or within the special maritime and territorial jurisdiction of the United States, or enters or leaves Indian country, with the intent to kill, injure, harass, or place under surveillance with intent to kill, injure, harass, or intimidate another person, and in the course of, or as a result of, such travel places that person in reasonable fear of the death of, or serious bodily injury to, or causes substantial emotional distress to that person, a member of the immediate family (as defined in section 115) of that person, or the spouse or intimate partner of that person; or
(2) with the intent--
(A) to kill, injure, harass, or place under surveillance with intent to kill, injure, harass, or intimidate, or cause substantial emotional distress to a person in another State or tribal jurisdiction or within the special maritime and territorial jurisdiction of the United States; or
(B) to place a person in another State or tribal jurisdiction, or within the special maritime and territorial jurisdiction of the United States, in reasonable fear of the death of, or serious bodily injury to--
(i) that person;
(ii) a member of the immediate family (as defined in section 115) of that person; or
(iii) a spouse or intimate partner of that person;
uses the mail, any interactive computer service, or any facility of interstate or foreign commerce to engage in a course of conduct that causes substantial emotional distress to that person or places that person in reasonable fear of the death of, or serious bodily injury to, any of the persons described in clauses (i) through (iii) of subparagraph (B);
shall be punished as provided in section 2261(b) of this title.

§ 2261A. Stalking
2013 Reauthorization, enacted legislation
Whoever--
(1) travels in interstate or foreign commerce or is present within the special maritime and territorial jurisdiction of the United States, or enters or leaves Indian country, with the intent to kill, injure, harass, intimidate, or place under surveillance with intent to kill, injure, harass, or intimidate another person, and in the course of, or as a result of, such travel or presence engages in conduct that—
(A) places that person in reasonable fear of the death of, or serious bodily injury to--
(i) that person;
(ii) an immediate family member (as defined in section 115) of that person; or
(iii) a spouse or intimate partner of that person; or
(B) causes, attempts to cause, or would be reasonably expected to cause substantial emotional distress to a person described in clause (i), (ii), or (iii) of subparagraph (A); or
(2) with the intent to kill, injure, harass, intimidate, or place under surveillance with intent to kill, injure, harass, or intimidate another person, uses the mail, any interactive computer service or electronic communication service or electronic communication system of interstate commerce, or any other facility of interstate or foreign commerce to engage in a course of conduct that—
(A) places that person in reasonable fear of the death of or serious bodily injury to a person described in clause (i), (ii), or (iii) of paragraph (1)(A); or
(B) causes, attempts to cause, or would be reasonably expected to cause substantial emotional distress to a person described in clause (i), (ii), or (iii) of paragraph (1)(A),
shall be punished as provided in section 2261(b) of this title.

Under the revised stalking statute, courts may consider acts that "would be reasonably expected to cause substantial emotional distress" as stalking. Conversely, under the 2006 statute, the substantial emotional distress must actually occur or manifest in the victim.

"Stalking traditionally takes the form of unwanted direct and/or indirect contact, but now 26 percent of stalking victims experience cyberstalking—unwanted contact or monitoring through electronic devices..."[28] As such, VAWA 2013 adds two new media through which sufficiently threatening communication may trigger the statute: electronic communication service or electronic communication system of interstate commerce.

E. INTENSIFIES FOCUS ON SEXUAL ASSAULT

VAWA 2013 directs additional resources on sexual assault prevention, enforcement, and services. It expands the definition of sexual assault to include instances in which "the victim lacks capacity to consent." It seeks to improve law enforcement responses to sexual assault and to address the backlog of untested rape kits. Lawmakers identified this backlog as an affront to justice, as simple DNA analysis could lead to many arrests; consequently, Congress incorporated the Sexual Assault Forensic Evidence Reporting (SAFER) Act of 2013 into the reauthorization. The SAFER Act authorizes the attorney general to provide funding for state and local governments to audit forensic evidence backlogs, and creates a national reporting system to expedite their processing. Additionally, the act requires the director of the FBI to develop protocols for the accurate and efficient collection and processing of DNA evidence, and provide training and technical assistance to state and local governments in the implementation of these protocols.

F. EXTENDS PROTECTIONS TO LESBIAN, GAY, BISEXUAL, AND TRANSGENDER (LGBT) SURVIVORS:

New inclusive language in the act provides the LGBT community with access to many of the same abuse and trauma services available to heterosexual survivors.

The VAWA 2013 reauthorization "ensures that lesbian, gay, bisexual, and transgender survivors have access to the services they need and deserve."[29] As the ACLU posits, "the need could not be clearer. Studies indicate that LGBT people experience domestic violence at roughly the same rate as the general population. However, it is estimated that less than one-in-five LGBT domestic violence victims receives help from a service provider and less than in one-in-ten victims reports violence to law enforcement."[30] And in those instances in which they do seek help, LGBT victims are often met with resistance. "In a 2010 survey, 45 percent of gay and transgender victims were turned away when they sought help from a domestic violence shelter, and 55 percent of those seeking protection orders were denied them."[31]

The reauthorization secures these protections in a number of ways. First, the act updates the definition of domestic violence to include those in relationships with an "intimate partner" as a protected class. Next, any recipient of VAWA grant funds agrees to a policy of nondiscrimination, which prohibits the denial of services on the basis of sexual identity or gender orientation. Third, the act expands the definitions of underserved populations to include those "who face barriers in accessing and using victim services" because of sexual orientation or gender identity. Last, VAWA 2013 makes a commitment to "developing, enlarging, or strengthening programs and projects to provide services and responses targeting male and female victims of domestic violence, dating violence, sexual assault, or stalking, whose ability to access traditional services and responses is affected by their sexual orientation or gender identity..."

G. INFORMS AND EMPOWERS COLLEGE STUDENTS:

In addition to sex offenses, colleges and universities must now also report incidents of domestic violence, dating violence, and stalking, under an amended Clery Act. Further, schools are required to take steps to prevent violence and provide resources and information to victims.

A large number of 18- to 25-year-old women reside on college campuses. "Women younger than 25 are at increased risk for sexual assault. More than 75 percent of women surveyed in the NISVS study who had been victims of a completed rape were first raped before their 25th birthday, with approximately 42 percent of these victims experiencing their first completed rape before the age of 18.[32] Additionally, "[s]tudies have shown that one in five women will be the victim of an attempted or completed sexual assault while they are in college."[33]

VAWA 2013 requires that colleges and universities subject to the Clery Act[34] (1) report domestic violence, dating violence, and stalking, in addition to sex offenses; (2) offer preventative training programs; and (3) adopt certain procedures pertaining to investigating these crimes and notifying relevant parties.

Reporting Requirements: "Institutions subject to the Clery Act must distribute an Annual Security Report to current and prospective students and employees that contains campus crime statistics for the previous three calendar years, as well as policies and procedures pertaining to campus security."[35] Prior to VAWA 2013, institutions only had to report statistics on forcible and non-forcible sex crimes and aggravated assault. The reauthorization adds the requirement that if an incident of domestic violence, dating violence, or stalking was reported to campus security or the police, then the institution must report it, under the Clery Act. Additionally, institutions must report "hate crimes" – or crimes in which the perpetrator selected the victim based on perceived characteristics. VAWA 2013 adds "national origin" and "gender identity" to the category of protected traits. Last, for crimes deemed to be a threat to others, the institution must withhold the name of the victim(s). These requirements go into effect on March 7, 2014, one year after the enactment of the reauthorization.

Training Requirements: Under the reauthorization, institutions must offer new students and new employees training programs that raise awareness of rape, domestic violence, dating violence, sexual assault, and stalking. These programs must include: (1) definitions of the applicable offenses and consent; (2) options for safe bystander intervention; (3) warning signs of abusive behavior; (4) a statement from the institution stating its prohibition of applicable offenses; (5) ongoing prevention and awareness campaigns.

Procedural Requirements: Institutions must now provide students with information about victims' options concerning notification of, and assistance from, police and campus security, as well as victim rights and institution responsibilities concerning protective orders. Further, VAWA

2013 provides lengthy guidance on the standards institutions must follow during investigations and disciplinary proceedings concerning domestic violence, dating violence, sexual assault, and stalking cases.

H. EXTENDS PROTECTION AND JUSTICE TO NATIVE AMERICANS:

Tribal courts now have jurisdiction over non-Native offenders who commit domestic violence, dating violence, or violate a protective order while on tribal land.

VAWA 2013 offers protection to Native American women, who, as a group, experience disproportionately high rates of violence. A nationwide study found that one third of Native American women will be raped in their lifetime.[36] Another study found that three out of five have been the victim of domestic violence.[37] "Native American women are almost three times as likely to be raped or sexually assaulted as all other races in the United States ... Additionally, while violence against white and African-American victims is primarily intra-racial, nearly four in five American Indian victims of rape and sexual assault described their offender as white."[38]

Prior to the reauthorization, if a Native American woman was raped or assaulted by a non-Indian on tribal land, she must complain to federal authorities, as "tribal courts have no authority at all to prosecute a non-Indian, even if he lives on the reservation and is married to a tribal member."[39] Unfortunately, "[f]or a host of reasons, the current legal structure for prosecuting domestic violence in Indian country is not well-suited to combating this pattern of escalating violence. Federal resources, which are often the only ones that can investigate and prosecute these crimes, are often far away and stretched thin."[40]

To address this "epidemic … cycle of violence,"[41] under VAWA 2013 "[t]ribes will be able to exercise their sovereign power to investigate, prosecute, convict, and sentence both Indians and non-Indians who assault Indian spouses or dating partners or violate a protection order in Indian country."[42] This power to criminally prosecute non-Indian offenders takes effect in March 2015 or sooner if the tribe participates in the Justice Department's Pilot Project.[43] Additionally, tribes are now immediately able to issue and enforce civil protection orders. This criminal jurisdiction over non-Indians is concurrent with state/federal jurisdictions, and will extend to domestic violence, dating violence, and criminal violations of protection orders. However, tribes will not have jurisdiction over crimes between two non-Indians or strangers, crimes committed outside of Indian country, crimes committed by a person with no ties to the tribe, and child or elder abuse not involving the violation of a protection order. Further, under VAWA 2013, tribes have certain obligations. The tribal court must: protect the rights of the non-Indian defendant, pursuant to the Indian Civil Rights Act of 1968 and the Tribal Law and Order Act of 2010; include non-Indians in jury pools; and inform the defendant of his/her right to file a Federal habeas corpus petition. To offset the cost of implementation of this program, tribal governments will receive a total of $25 million in federal grants for fiscal years 2014 to 2018, and may also allocate funds they receive from DOJ Coordinated Tribal Assistance Solicitation grants for this purpose. Participation in the program, however, is completely voluntary.

1. Choose one change in VAWA. Compare and contrast the update with the original bill.

2. According to the author, what other changes could be made to make VAWA stronger?

CHAPTER 5

WHAT THE MEDIA SAYS

The media shapes the dialogue we have about sexual harassment and gender violence. It shares stories from around the world of the people impacted by these issues and the people trying to make a difference. It also provides important historical and political context for cases. The media often serves as a direct link to those who are comfortable sharing their stories, which gives a face to the issues while letting the subjects share their own thoughts. For women who may be marginalized, this kind of access is crucial to helping the public understand how other issues intersect with harassment and gender violence to create toxic situations. The media is also able to highlight contradictions in how we treat these issues, point to possible solutions, and make sure the discussion is accessible to people with all levels of knowledge. The shared narratives help us connect with and understand victims on a human level, rather than simply as statistics.

"NEW DOCUMENTARY USES ART TO RESIST SEXUAL HARASSMENT IN EGYPT" BY MIRIAM ELBA, FROM *WAGING NONVIOLENCE*, OCTOBER 8, 2014

An upcoming documentary film, "The People's Girls," has become one of the latest efforts to combat gender violence in Egypt. The film follows three Egyptians — one young male "tuk tuk" driver and two young women — through their experiences with sexual harassment and how they are fighting the dominant patriarchal views that are still prevalent in Egypt.

The film's creators, Tinne Van Loon and Colette Ghunim, stated that their inspiration to make this film came from their own experiences as students in Egypt and a desire to show what average Egyptian women endure on a daily basis. Van Loon said, "It often deters us, like many other women, to walk outside or take public transportation, seeing as we don't want to deal with the intimidation and anxiety. Everywhere we've been in the world — the United States, Latin America, Europe, South Asia — we've experienced various levels of sexual harassment."

The title of the film, "The People's Girls," carries a heavy and significant meaning. In an interview with the blog Egyptian Streets, Ghunim explained, "[In Arabic] the saying is commonly used to describe a well-mannered, cultured, respectable girl ... When people blame victims ... they often argue that if only the girl was a 'people's girl' then she wouldn't get harassed."

Last month, a short video Ghunim created entitled "Creepers on the Bridge" went viral. It showed, from the camera's point of view, the uncomfortable and even predatory looks she would get when crossing a highly trafficked bridge in Cairo.

In advance of the release of the full documentary, Ghunim and Van Loon have published six excerpts that show the wide spectrum of experiences, thoughts and opinions on sexual harassment. One woman named Sahar spoke of her frustration that, despite the fact that she wears a niqab, she still gets verbally harassed by men when going out. Another girl named Asmaa explains why she believes women are partially to blame for being harassed. If these videos are any indication, the film looks like it will be a multifaceted portrait of life for Egyptian women in public spaces.

1. What role can film play in helping us understand sexual harassment and gender violence?

2. Do you think it is important to understand how these issues impact countries around the world? Why or why not?

"WHAT ARE MEN DOING TO CHALLENGE AND STOP GENDER VIOLENCE?" BY VICTORIA LAW, FROM *WAGING NONVIOLENCE*, NOVEMBER 5, 2014

I've been writing a lot about domestic violence this fall, both in the wake of the publicity surrounding Ray Rice's beating of his then-fiancée Janay Palmer and because

October was Domestic Violence Awareness Month. As I've rifled through my files to dig out examples of community organizing against gender violence, I've realized that most of the examples concentrate on women organizing against gender violence. This made me wonder: What are men doing to challenge gender violence, both individually in their daily lives and collectively as part of their political organizing? So I began asking that question on Twitter. I have a bunch of followers who are male-identified, so I figured they'd all chime in and we'd have a mini-discussion, right?

Wrong. Instead, I started noticing that people were unfollowing me. To be fair, not all of them may have done so because of my constant variation of the question: "MEN (cis and trans): What are you doing to challenge #DV (individually or collectively)?" appearing in their stream every other day. But the near-silence that met my question every time I sent it out was more than a little unnerving. While I don't personally know all my followers, I do know some of them, including men who identify as feminist or say that they don't put up with violence against women. I figured that, at the very least, they would speak up, right?

Wrong again. No one I know responded. (I did get two responses from people I don't know. I'm very thankful that they responded.)

Around this time, I was asked to write a piece for *Jacobin* critiquing carceral feminism, which is the kind of feminism that sees an increased police response, prosecution and harsher prison sentences as the solution to gender violence. While writing the piece, I started becoming annoyed that when we (radicals, anarchists, communists, socialists, what-have-you types of leftists) talk about domestic violence and problematic ways of addressing it, we tend to direct our anger towards carceral feminists, pointing out all the ways in which policing and increased criminalized responses have placed marginalized women at increased risk of state violence.

But we rarely seem to look in our own circles and ask, "Well, what are *we* doing to create alternatives to relying on the state to stop domestic violence?" Why is this only a discussion among feminists (and feminist women at that)? Where is the rest of our so-called movement in these discussions and in these actions? Why isn't challenging domestic violence, abuse and other forms of gender violence incorporated into our social justice organizing and into the beliefs that we're espousing?

I'm not trying to say that no one is doing work on this front. After all, I did get three responses to my repeated Twitter question over the course of a month, and there are a couple of recent examples of men addressing gendered violence.

In 2010, after a rash of muggings and robberies in the Bedford-Stuyvesant neighborhood of Brooklyn, men in the neighborhood decided they needed to take action. They formed a group called We Make Us Better and began escorting people home from the subway station, making it less likely that people would be targeted. But they didn't stop there. The group also sponsored a neighborhood outreach walk, stopping to talk to young men hanging out on corners and encouraging them to become involved in their community. The following year, the group provided prom tuxedos for the 30 graduating senior men at the local high school. To get a tuxedo, the young men had to attend a course on etiquette before the prom. While the idea of an etiquette course may conjure up images of great-aunt Millie telling you which fork to use or the proper way to eat shellfish, that wasn't this course.

"We want to re-establish a positive male influence in our community," Titus Mitchell, a co-founder of We Make Us Better, told NBC New York. "A lot of these kids don't know how to open the door for a young lady or tie a tie. If they don't have any male figures around, how will they ever learn?"

I'm not sure if the group is still active. Both their Twitter and Facebook pages show no activity since 2012. In the face of the neighborhood's rapid gentrification, it's possible that some got priced out, others moved away and overall momentum for the group faded. But what we can take away from this group's example is that, for over a year, men in the neighborhood acted to not only prevent the immediate threats of violence that targeted women, but also begin to address underlying assumptions about masculinity and acceptable male behavior in their own communities.

Last year, utilizing October as Domestic Violence Awareness Month, Emotional Justice Unplugged, the Chicago Taskforce on Violence against Girls and Women, and Free Marissa Now launched a month-long letter writing campaign called #31forMARISSA. The campaign urged men to write letters of support to Marissa Alexander, a Florida mother who was arrested after firing a warning shot to keep her abusive husband from continuing to attack her. Although her conviction had been overturned in September 2013, she was still in prison the following month. Eventually, she was released on bail; the prosecutor has vowed to seek a 60-year sentence against her when they go to trial in December 2014.

The campaign #31forMARISSA urged men to share stories of violence experienced by the women in their own circles, donate funds for her trial fees and become engaged as active allies in the domestic violence movement. Their letters were posted on a Tumblr while paper copies were printed and mailed to Alexander each week. Over 100 people responded to the call.

This year's campaign is entitled #31forRay and asks men to write about childhood experiences witnessing domestic violence, its impact, and the actions of men in their family and community to stop the violence. Interestingly, this particular call seems to have garnered much less participation. There were two letters when I checked. Hopefully, by the time this column is published, there will be many more.

Addressing domestic violence and other forms of gender violence need to be seen not just as a women's issue. We can continue to be angry at carceral feminists' reliance on policing and imprisonment as the solution to gender violence, but until *everyone* in our communities takes steps to create and implement alternative responses, people will continue to see that as the default solution.

So let me throw down the gauntlet and challenge all men to take concrete actions towards ending gender violence, both in their individual lives and in their political organizing work. It's not going to be a short and sweet task, but if we truly are committed to transforming our world, then we need to make those commitments.

1. What can men do to help combat gender violence and sexual harassment?

2. According to this article, should men take a lead role in fighting these issues? Do you agree? Why or why not?

"CHIAPAS WOMEN WORK TOWARD A 'LIFE FREE OF VIOLENCE'" BY LAURIE LILES, FROM THE *CRONKITE NEWS* BORDERLANDS PROJECT, SEPTEMBER 25, 2014

SAN CRISTÓBAL DE LAS CASAS, Mexico – When a pending downpour forced Lesvia Entzin Gomez to return to her mother-in-law's without the apples she had left to cut, her drunken, enraged husband pulled out a shotgun.

"I did not think he had a shell in the shotgun," Entzin Gomez recalled. "I thought he was playing ... then he pointed it at me and I heard it go off. He shot me in the face and my eyes."

The July 15, 2013, attack left the 24-year-old mother of three blind and suffering from headaches and dizziness. Her husband, Jorge Navarro Hernandez, remains in jail, but she said she has been threatened by his relatives and is in constant fear for her life.

Her case is not unusual: 30 percent of women in Chiapas state age 15 and older were victims of domestic violence in 2011, according to Mexico's most recent National Survey on the Dynamics of Relationships in the Household.

And while that seems shockingly high, Chiapas actually has the lowest domestic violence rate among Mexico's 31 states and federal district. The state of Mexico was highest at 56.9 percent. Nationally, 46.1 percent of Mexico's 42.6 million women reported physical, emotional or psychological abuse in the 2011 survey.

In Chiapas, where more than 70 percent live in poverty, activists say gender-based violence resulted in the deaths of 84 women from January to October 2013. Entzin Gomez narrowly missed becoming one of those statistics.

TELLING HER STORY

She told her story at a news conference nearly eight months after she was shot. Entzin Gomez kept her eyes downcast and her face partially shrouded beneath a gray woven shawl. Her scars were still visible and she moved slowly with the aid of a companion.

She was flanked by two members of Mexico President Enrique Peña Nieto's Executive Commission for Victims, who said they planned to take Entzin Gomez to Mexico City for medical treatment. But Entzin Gomez said she needed food and a safe place to live with her children.

"Right now we are suffering. We are eating just a little beans and corn," she said.

State and local officials have failed Entzin Gomez and her family, said Dr. Julio Barros Hernandez, one of the commissioners at the news conference.

"In this case, they have left Lesvia totally defenseless, depriving her of the essential rights that allow one to live with dignity," he said.

The other commissioner, Jaime del Rincon Rochin, said her plight is all too common.

"Lesvia is a painful example of the state in which many women are left when they survive an attack of femicide," del Rincon Rochin said. "What Lesvia is living through today is what many women live through in many parts of this country, and we cannot permit that this keeps happening."

Femicide – the act of killing a woman because of her gender – is a federal offense in Mexico, punishable by 40 to 60 years in prison, according to the U.S. State Department's Mexico 2013 Human Rights Report.

Twenty-eight states, including Chiapas and the federal district, have criminalized femicide and domestic abuse, but problems persist.

According to a 2012 report published by the Mexico Secretary of Governance, the number of female homicide victims increased dramatically over the previous three years, particularly in the federal district and eight states, including Chiapas.

And domestic abuse rates may be understated. Domestic violence victims from rural and indigenous communities often do not report abuse, said the State Department report, for fear of reprisal, of the stigma associated with domestic violence or because they may belong to communities where abuse is accepted.

As a result, the report said no authoritative government statistics are available on the number of abusers prosecuted, convicted or punished.

In Chiapas, the fight against domestic violence and for equal treatment has been going on longer than in most states in Mexico.

A REVOLUTIONARY NOTION

When indigenous rebels known as the EZLN – the Zapatistas – rebelled against the Mexican government on Jan. 1, 1994, the leftist group unveiled a Women's Revolutionary Law as a key feature of their manifesto, the First Declaration of the Lacandon Jungle. It's essentially a 10-article bill of rights for indigenous women.

The articles declare that women have a right to participate in the political system and hold leadership posts; to decide whom to marry and how many children to bear; to a fair wage and quality health care; and to a life free from sexual and domestic violence.

Author and researcher Hilary Klein said that to appreciate what has changed since the Zapatista rebellion you must first understand how cruel life was for indigenous women 30 years ago.

"Women lived in extremely oppressive situations where, in the public sphere and the private sphere, there was an extraordinary level of domestic violence and alcohol abuse," said Klein, who lived and worked with Zapatista women from 1997 to 2003.

Klein's book, "Compañeras: Zapatista Women's Stories," slated for release in January, documents what she calls the "seismic" transformation women in Zapatista territory experienced before, during and after the 1994 EZLN uprising.

Before the Zapatistas, Klein said, women had no control over their lives.

"They basically had to ask their husbands or their fathers for permission to leave the house," she said. "They were married very young and had children throughout their reproductive years."

As the Zapatistas began to mobilize in the 1980s, Roman Catholic Church leaders inspired by liberation theology influenced the movement, Klein said. Bishop Samuel Ruiz Garcia of the Diocese of San Cristobal de las Casas urged better treatment of women as he helped organize indigenous communities.

"As these leaders were saying, 'It's not OK for women to be treated this way,' there was a simultaneous push from the women themselves, who said they wanted things to change," Klein said.

She said the Zapatistas emphasized women's involvement as a way to grow their movement. EZLN leaders "pushed from the beginning that women can participate at all levels of the organization, and that has been their driving strategy to make changes around women's rights," Klein said.

The Zapatista attack on San Cristóbal de las Casas in 1994 was planned and led by Comandanta Ana Maria. Nearly 30 percent of insurgents were women, and Comandanta Ramona was the sole Zapatista representative at the First National Indian Congress in Mexico City in 1995.

In the years leading up to the rebellion, EZLN activist Susana traveled to dozens of villages throughout Chiapas collecting suggestions from thousands of indigenous women, according to Klein and other Zapatista historians. Their ideas were ultimately incorporated into the Women's Revolutionary Law.

"No event has been more important for the women's movement in Chiapas than the public appearance of the EZLN in 1994," author and Professor R. Aida Hernandez Castillo

wrote in "Contemporary Women's Movements in Chiapas."
Hernandez Castillo said the Zapatista movement and the
Women's Revolutionary Law were catalysts, prompting
indigenous women throughout Mexico to organize.

THE MOVEMENT STALLS

But Klein and local women's leaders say the explosive
period of female empowerment of the 1990s has plateaued
in recent years.

Human-rights activists' frustration was evident March
8 at an International Women's Day news conference and
protest rally that drew about 200 near the base of the large
Mayan cross facing the Cathedral of San Cristóbal de Las
Casas.

Organizers said the federal and state governments
have failed to protect Chiapas women from domestic
violence and femicide.

"Violence in Chiapas is extreme," said Center for
Women's Rights leader Alma Padilla Garcia in an interview.
"All forms of violence, poverty, hunger, all can be considered violence against women. We give responsibility for
this violence to the state of Mexico."

Federal and state officials in December launched
a domestic-violence prevention program that Chiapas
Attorney General Raciel Lopez Salazar says has reduced the
number of femicides and crimes committed against women.

In a March 8 statement, the attorney general's
office announced a 78 percent decrease in femicide
during the first quarter of 2014 compared with the same
period in 2013, from nine cases to two. It attributed
the reduction to a new program, the Emerging Action

Plan for the Prevention and Treatment of Femicide and Gender Violence. The office also said crimes against women declined by 58 percent during the same period.

Coordinated by Mexico's Secretary of Governance, the Ministry for Development and Empowerment of Women and the Chiapas attorney general's office, the initiative includes domestic-violence prevention workshops, media education, law-enforcement training and a 24-hour, toll-free domestic-abuse hotline.

Despite such initiatives, human-rights leaders say complex economic and social challenges continue to thwart progress and threaten women's safety.

Longtime women's rights activist Mercedes Bustamante Olivera, a founder of the Center for Research and Action for Latin Women, said women in Chiapas suffer under a "structure of violence" and male oppression.

"Because the capitalist system is organized on the basis of male parameters," she said, "men are aggressive toward women."

Discrimination against women leads to violence in family and personal relationships that leave women defenseless, Bustamante Olivera said. In order for change to occur, she said women must lead.

"Far from being victims, we take action," she said.

WOMEN LEAD THE FIGHT

A growing number of indigenous women in Chiapas are taking action. Pascuala Perez Gutierrez and Margarita Vasquez Boloma work with the Fray Pedro de la Nada Committee for Human Rights, an organization founded shortly after the 1994 uprising to train indigenous people about their fundamental rights.

Perez Gutierrez, 49, said after the violence and repression that led to the Zapatista rebellion, she and other indigenous women responded by organizing and educating themselves about their rights.

"Through this process, we found the need to participate," she said in an interview at the Center for Research and Action for Latin Women. "There were no spaces for women, so we found the need to organize, to participate, and to be valued as women."

Vasquez Boloma, 19, grew up in the Zapatista community of Nueva Jeruselen. She is a trainer with Fray Pedro, educating women and men in workshops as part of a 14-month gender-equality education program.

She said violence against women is widespread. But through training, women are learning to defend themselves.

"Violence comes from everywhere ... there isn't a space where you can say there is no violence," Vasquez Boloma said. "In the house, in the streets, everywhere there is violence. Now that we're receiving workshops, we're going to defend ourselves."

Perez Gutierrez and Vasquez Boloma said men have mixed reactions to women receiving this training. Some are hostile to the idea of women defending themselves.

"They don't like it," Perez Gutierrez said. "They think especially the promoters, they're going to put bad ideas in the heads of women. There's even threats because they don't feel that it's right for the women to defend themselves."

Vasquez Boloma sees the same reaction in her community.

"When they hold a workshop and a woman speaks, the men don't respect her," she said. "Some men think that only men should decide."

Others have come around to the idea.

"Some men have received training and they support us," Vasquez Boloma said. "So things are getting better with men, too."

Perez Gutierrez said she's seen progress in the 21 years she's been fighting for women in Chiapas. The Women's Revolutionary Law helped liberate women, she said.

"I don't have to ask anybody for permission," she said. "Nobody asks me, 'Where are you going?' I make my own decision to leave or to go. I think that's change."

Both women look to future generations to continue the struggle for women's rights in Chiapas.

If she has a daughter someday, Vasquez Boloma envisions for her a dignified life and a tranquil state of mind. Beyond that, she said she has only one wish.

"That she would live free of violence."

1. How are women leading the fight against gender violence and harassment in Chiapas, Mexico?

2. Using what you have learned about these issues, compare and contrast the situation in Chiapas with that in the United States.

"THE VISA CURSE" BY DIANA ANAHI TORRES, FROM *OTHERWORDS*, DECEMBER 30, 2014

Many American women are still told they have to choose between love and career. But for many immigrants, that outdated dilemma is legally enforced.

"I am here legally but I don't have the right to work or even open an independent bank account," Rashi Bhatnagar, an accomplished journalist from India, told me recently.

Bhatnagar began working for Magna Publications, one of India's largest and oldest publishing houses, a month after getting her Master's degree. But when she got married to a U.S. visa holder in 2009, everything changed.

Every year, the United States gives 85,000 H1-B visas to highly skilled foreign workers, such as engineers and information technologists. The workers don't travel alone. They often bring their spouses and children in tow on H-4 visas.

These visas give holders, most of whom are women, the right to live legally in the United States. But they come with serious caveats.

Most significantly, they deny their holders the right to a social security number and legal employment. This places women in extremely vulnerable positions.

Bhatnagar admits that she knew about the restrictions before she migrated to the United States. Yet the alternative — staying behind to pursue her career away from her husband — simply wasn't an option for her. So she moved to the United States and placed her career on hold.

Even so, the new mother says she's one of the lucky ones. She's happily married, and her husband encourages her to pursue her hobbies and interests.

Many others face harsher circumstances. Through a blog and Facebook page she runs called "H-4 Visa, a Curse," Bhatnagar has discovered thousands of immigrant women who suffer from severe depression, domestic abuse, or feelings of [having] lost [their] identity.

"I was a researcher in a renowned government research institute in India," recalled Harpreer Kaur, a former molecular biologist from India in one post. "But in the U.S. I became a house maker... I have to ask my husband for every small thing."

"All my talent is getting wasted because of my visa status," laments Chethana Manjunath, who — in India — was a doctor who specialized in internal medicine and clinical pathology. "I am losing my self confidence."

As the stories from Bhatnagar's blog attest, many of these women are highly educated but can't contribute to the U.S. economy through paid work. And that's a huge loss.

If women like Manjunath could work, for example, one study estimated that they could each add an additional 9.4 jobs, $773,655 in total wages and benefits, and $45,665 in local and state tax revenue per year.

H-4 visas also make women more vulnerable to domestic abuse.

One woman, for instance, revealed that if she accused her husband of domestic abuse, she risked losing her children and her right to reside legally in the United States. Her fear has kept her silent for years.

Scores of other women share her story.

In November, President Barack Obama finally addressed this issue through his executive action on immigration.

Though better known for granting undocumented residents a reprieve from deportation, the order also included a provision that grants the right to work legally in the United States to spouses of H1-B workers — if they've already applied for their green cards.

This will immediately affect an estimated 100,000 H-4 visa holders and an estimated 30,000 more each year from now.

Bhatnagar is quick to point out that this isn't enough.

"There are many children who are also here on H-4 visas," she says. "But if they turn 21 before their parents receive their green cards, they will be forced to return to India. There are also thousands of women on H-4 visas who are not yet eligible to apply for their green cards. Congress needs to address their needs too."

Congress should take these stories into account. Allowing these women to work and be economically independent isn't just good economic policy — it's a moral imperative.

1. How does immigration status impact women's ability to protect themselves from sexual harassment and gender violence?

2. What could the government do to better protect these women?

"DOMESTIC VIOLENCE: EFFORTS FOCUS ON GETTING GUNS AWAY FROM ABUSERS" BY BRITTANY ELENA MORRIS AND ALLISON GRINER, FROM *NEWS21*, AUGUST 16, 2014

Driving home from work on Sept. 11, 2008, Sarah Engle's mouth watered for her mom's lasagna. But instead of the smell of marinara sauce wafting from the kitchen to greet her, something grim was waiting.

"When I walked through the door, there was a rifle in my face. 'You take another step, I will shoot and kill you now,' James, my ex-boyfriend, said to me … even firing off a shot to prove the gun worked," she said.

He forced her into the bedroom at gunpoint and sexually assaulted her repeatedly through most of the night and into the morning.

"When I jumped out of bed, he shot me in the face." Advocates for domestic violence prevention and victims repeatedly asked Congress and state legislatures for a more streamlined process to keep guns out of the hands of abusers. However, the National Rifle Association and other gun rights groups argue firearm ownership and the Second Amendment are counterintuitive to such measures unless abusers have felony charges against them. They cite the necessity to arm oneself for protection against acts of violence.

A News21 investigation found that more people were murdered by intimate partners with guns than by criminals they didn't know.

Analysis of FBI data showed at least 3,464 people were shot to death in an act of domestic violence from 2008 to 2012, compared to 3,226 people killed in the same period — by guns or other means — by attackers they did not know or where the relationship to the victim was unknown.

"Everyone is surprised by the numbers," said Roberta Valente, a policy consultant for the National Domestic Violence Hotline. "Here they are, and we have solutions."

Six states — Louisiana, Minnesota, New Hampshire, Vermont, Wisconsin and Washington — passed laws to remove firearms from the homes of domestic abusers. Congress is considering at least four bills and Sen. Richard Blumenthal, D-Connecticut, said he plans to introduce a bill calling for national background checks on gun buyers.

"The Second Amendment is a guarantee of the Constitution. But no constitutional guarantee is absolute," Blumenthal said. "The two have to be bound — public safety and the safety of a potential victim of domestic violence and a Second Amendment right."

Along with Blumenthal's bills, the Senate Judiciary Committee held a July 30 hearing on domestic violence and firearms. Nearly two dozen victims from 16 states were in the audience.

The new law in Wisconsin came too late for Engle.

She woke hours after the attack, oblivious to the blood trickling below her left eye, down her cheek and onto her T-shirt. She felt sluggish and struggled to put one foot in front of the other as she looked around the house she shared in Prentice with her mom, Charlotte Engle. Her ex-boyfriend was gone, along with her car, and the phone lines were cut.

She paused and thought: Where is my mom?

The doorway to Charlotte Engle's room was barricaded with the green couch from the living room. Sarah Engle could barely muster the strength to pull it away from the wall to slip inside.

"I saw my mom sitting on the floor. She was very relaxed almost. She wasn't taped or anything. I grabbed her hand and I remember it was very cold. I said 'Mom, I am going to go get help. I am going to get help!'"

Shoeless, she walked, fell, then crawled down their gravel driveway and onto the road. She flagged down a truck. The driver's eyes were big as he took in her face, immediately taking her to the nearest clinic.

James LaHoud, 41, shot and killed Charlotte Engle that night in 2008, and left her daughter, now 40, with scars she will bear for the rest of her life. The worst of them, she said, is the thought that everything might have been prevented.

She filed a temporary order of protection against LaHoud the first year into their relationship after he threw a shoe at her. LaHoud was barred from owning or possessing a firearm until May 11, 2009, exactly eight months after Charlotte Engle's death.

His first wife and an ex-girlfriend previously filed for protective orders against LaHoud, who also faced dropped domestic violence charges — all before he met Sarah Engle.

"He shouldn't have had a gun at all. He didn't have a gun permit, didn't go through a background check and didn't have gun safety training of any kind," she said.

LaHoud is currently serving life plus 80 years in a Wisconsin prison.

Engle is part of a growing community of victims.

Melanie Lyon ran away from from her abusive ex-husband, Ronald Lee Haskell, 33. On July 16 he followed Lyon to Spring, Texas, where he dressed as a FedEx worker and forced his way into the home of her sister, Katie Stay, looking for his wife.

He held Stay, her husband and five children at gunpoint and killed all but one family member execution-style when they wouldn't disclose where Lyon was hiding. Cassidy Stay, 5, played dead and called 911 after Haskell left. Lyon was not in the home at the time of the shootings.

Haskell had a history of domestic violence. He allegedly beat Lyon in front of their children, dragging her by her hair around their home in Logan, Utah. He was arrested in 2008 for domestic violence, and Lyon filed an order of protection in 2013 in the midst of their divorce.

"The right to bear arms is not more important than protecting a woman's life," said Valente, the violence hotline policy consultant. "Right now what we have isn't enough."

Haskell is in jail awaiting trial for the murders of the Stay family.

In a survey taken over eight weeks this spring 2014 by the National Domestic Violence Hotline, 16 percent of the 4,721 anonymous callers to the hotline said their partners had access to a gun and it frightened them.

When Congress reauthorized the Violence Against Women Act last year, it included a provision that keeps most people from buying or possessing firearms while subject to full protective orders filed by intimate partners. At the insistence of the gun lobby, the law does not allow confiscation of guns from people under temporary orders, since they have not a chance to challenge the order in court.

Each state determines the duration of gun confiscations under the law and where relinquished firearms go. In some cases, the sheriff's department holds the guns; in others it's a family member.

In California, anyone served with a temporary protective order has 24 hours to turn over any weapons. In San Mateo County, south of San Francisco, authorities ensure firearms are removed from subject homes. On the other end of the spectrum, Kentucky passed a law to expedite concealed carry permits for victims of domestic violence.

Chelsea Parsons co-authored two Center for American Progress studies on the deadly effects of guns in homes with domestic violence, research that contributed to state legislation on the issue. She said it's important "for voices from the advocacy world to get involved and really make sure that law enforcement and lawmakers are developing policies and practices."

Things were looking up for Courtney Weaver in January 2010. Her breakup with her boyfriend had turned into a surprise engagement and the holidays the 23-year-old had spent alone in her Arcata, California, apartment were behind her.

Not everything was perfect. The possessive boyfriend was now her possessive fiance, so on Jan. 15, 2010, she planned to take a break by attending the concert of a friend and fellow blues musician.

She said she was putting on makeup when she heard rustling. Her fiance, Kenneth Fiaui had been attacked by her cat. She heard him cock his gun.

She had to get him water. Anything to calm him down, keep him inside, where he wouldn't hurt anyone.

"I was talking with him, trying to figure out what was going on and understand what he was planning on doing with his gun," she said. He lunged for the kitchen door, where Weaver was standing. He fired.

A hollow-point bullet exploded through her right arm, passing straight into her right upper lip. Her jaw was shattered, she lost five teeth, and her tongue was cut in multiple places by bullet shards.

The initial surgeries to reconstruct her face and arm took 27 hours over the course of 12 days, after which, Weaver still had to return to her apartment to clean up her own blood. "It was so ... humiliating," she said.

As she lowered herself to the floor to mop up the blood, something caught her eye: guns left behind by her fiance, propped up against the fridge. The police did not take them.

The anger she felt followed her to Washington state, where she moved to complete her surgeries. She became a volunteer advocate in Washington's fight to pass stricter domestic violence laws.

Before this year, Washington state law let judges decide when and how a firearm should be removed from a home where domestic violence had occurred.

State Rep. Roger Goodman, a longtime advocate for reforming Washington's domestic violence laws, said new legislation was 12 years in the making. In 2010, Goodman convened a workgroup to forge a comprehensive package of bills that included taking firearms from people subject to protective orders, no-contact orders and restraining orders.

The package bill — the first of its kind in 30 years — passed, but without the firearm removal measure, which would allow a judge to order firearms out of the house of a domestic abuser.

He tried again in 2011, 2012 and 2013. The bill finally passed unanimously this year through Washington's Legislature.

"I didn't believe it," said Weaver, who attended the vote. "It took me a few weeks to actually believe that it was going to get signed into law."

Goodman called his bill "arguably the most important bill we passed this entire legislative session," even though he had to make concessions to opponents. The final version of the bill tightened the standards for gun seizure: A court must not only approve a protective order but find the accused to be a "credible threat" before ordering guns removed.

Goodman said the compromise was the only way to get the bill passed.

"I don't know if media attention and the testimony of victims made as much of a difference as the internal politics of the Legislature," he said. "This is an election year, and I don't think anyone running would like to be accused of allowing domestic abusers to keep their weapons."

National groups such as Moms Demand Action, Everytown for Gun Safety and Americans for Responsible Solutions combined their efforts with state advocates in a strategy that rebrands domestic-violence-related gun seizure as a public safety issue, rather than just taking guns.

Sarah Kenney, director of public policy for the Vermont Network Against Domestic and Sexual Violence, has been working on legislation since a 2009 state panel on domestic violence recommended that judges and police remove guns from abusers subject to protective orders.

Five years later, the provision — outlining a step-by-step process for enforcement — passed.

It was a notable success, Kenney said. Before, firearms advocacy was "political suicide." Now the dialogue is shaped around "community safety." The success, she said, is thanks in part to large-scale organizations "elevating the debate about violence against women and firearms at the national level."

While Everytown for Gun Safety has varying levels of engagement in each state, an official there said the organization is working at the grassroots level to help push for legislation.

"Here's what I know: We worked closely with domestic violence prevention advocates to help pass new laws in six states, and in all of those states, the laws passed either unanimously or nearly unanimously," said Brina Milikowsky, the Everytown director of strategy and partnership.

Those bills were bipartisan and signed by governors from both parties. Republican Gov. Scott Walker said Wisconsin's Stopping Abuse Fatalities through Enforcement Act will help the state "do better in protecting the victims, and potential victims, of domestic abuse and connect them with crucial services, when they need our help the most."

Riding this wave, national groups and advocates are now looking at closing loopholes in the federal law that leave domestic violence victims vulnerable to dating partners and stalkers. They account "overwhelmingly" for the number of domestic homicides in the U.S., said Parsons of the Center for American Progress, which has a record of at least 11,986 stalking convictions in 20 states.

A News21 analysis found that dating relationships accounted for at least 38 percent of homicides with a gun from 2008 to 2012.

Parsons co-authored "Women Under the Gun," which cites the Protecting Domestic Violence and Stalking Victims Act as one of the measures that might decrease the number of domestic homicides. The bill, sponsored by Sen. Amy Klobuchar, D-Minnesota, includes provisions that would restrict abusive dating partners' and stalkers' ability to own a gun.

The bill is stalled in Congress with no expected action this year. The National Rifle Association wrote senators in June saying Klobuchar's bill "manipulates emotionally compelling issues such as 'domestic violence' and 'stalking' simply to cast as wide a net as possible for federal firearm prohibitions."

Sarah Engle's scars from the day LaHoud shot her in 2008 are still obvious. The left side of her face is paralyzed. The bullet shattered the skull on the left side of her face.

Even with continuous speech and cognitive rehabilitation, Engle's memory will never quite be what it used to, and her speech slurs at times. Still, she has spent this year talking with other victims, writing columns and testifying in support of Wisconsin's SAFE Act.

The SAFE Act "gives teeth" to state and federal law, said state Sen. Jerry Petrowski, a co-sponsor. Under the law, courts can issue arrest warrants if accused abusers fail to surrender all their firearms.

One victory under her belt, Engle has set her sights on the national level. On June 18, she told her story to more than 200 people at the Corcoran Gallery of Art in Washington, D.C., sharing the stage with former

Congresswoman Gabrielle Giffords, an Arizona Democrat who was the victim of a high-profile shooting attack in Tucson in 2011.

Giffords was in town with the group she founded after her attack, Americans for Responsible Solutions, to deliver 37,000 petition signatures to the U.S. Senate asking for a hearing on domestic violence and firearms.

"Dangerous people with guns are a threat to women. Criminals with guns. Stalkers with guns. Abusers with guns. That makes gun violence a women's issue. For mothers. For families. For me and you," Giffords said.

Engle and Giffords snapped a photo together before they asked the audience to call their lawmakers and encourage them to pass Klobuchar's bill.

"I'll be here as long as they need me," Engle said. "Something good came from something so bad. [The SAFE Act] could be the beginning to the end of domestic violence in Wisconsin. Now we just need to work on the rest of the U.S."

1. How do guns impact harassment and gender violence in the United States?

2. How might we balance the right to bear arms with the protection of vulnerable populations?

CHAPTER 6

WHAT AVERAGE CITIZENS SAY

Public opinion is the driving force behind changes in how we address sexual harassment and gender violence. Pressure from average citizens shapes policy and the way the public understanding of these issues evolves mirrors the ways in which they are treated. While in the early twentieth century sexual harassment was considered a standard and expected experience among women, the decision of ordinary people to stand up for their right to be given privacy and respect was the first step in creating the laws that now protect women and men in the workplace, at home, and around the world. The opinions of average citizens are sometimes shaped more by personal experience than statistics or other research, which brings an important but limited dimension to the debate. In many ways, the public is a mirror that reflects back the sum of all efforts by advocacy groups, leaders, and the media who portray sexual harassment and gender violence.

"BERKELEY'S HANDLING OF SEXUAL HARASSMENT IS A DISGRACE" BY MICHAEL EISEN, FROM MICHAELEISEN.ORG, MARCH 10, 2016

What more is there to say?

Another case where a senior member of the Berkeley faculty, this time Berkeley Law Dean Sujit Choudhry, was found to have violated the campus's sexual harassment policy and was given a slap on the wrists by the administration. Astronomer Geoff Marcy's punishment for years of harassment of students was a talking to and a warning never to do it again, and now Choudhry was put on some kind of secret probation for a year, sent for additional training, and docked 10% of his meager $470,000 a year salary.

Despite a constant refrain from senior administrators that it takes cases of sexual harassment seriously, the administration's actions demonstrate that it does not. What is the point of having a sexual harassment policy if violations of it have essentially no sanctions? Through its responses to Marcy and Choudhry, it is now clear that the university views sexual harassment by its senior male faculty not as what it is – an inexcusable abuse of power that undermines the university's entire mission and has a severe negative effect on our students and staff – but rather as a mistake that some faculty make because they don't know better.

If the university wants to show that it is serious about ending sexual harassment on campus, then it has to take cases of sexual harassment seriously. This means being unambiguous about what is and is not acceptable behavior and real consequences when people violate the rules. Faculty and administrators who engage in harassing behavior don't do it by accident. They make a choice to engage in behavior they either know is wrong or have no excuse for not knowing is wrong. And, at Berkeley at least, they do so knowing that if they get caught, the university will respond by saying, "Bad boy. Don't do that again. We're watching you now." Does [anyone] think this is an actual deterrent?

Through its handling of the Marcy, Choudhry and other cases, the Berkeley administration has shown utter contempt for the welfare of its students and staff. It has shown that it views its job not to create an optimal environment for education by ensuring that faculty behavior is consistent with the university's mission, but rather to protect faculty, especially famous ones, from the consequences of their actions.

It is now clear that excuse making and wrist slapping in response to sexual harassment is so endemic in the Berkeley administration that it might as well be official policy. And just like there is no excuse for sexual[ly] harassing students and staff, there is no excuse for sanctioning this kind of behavior. It's time for the administrators – all of them – who have repeatedly failed the campus community on this issue to go. It's the only way forward.

1. What about Berkeley's handling of sexual harassment allegations does the author take issue with?

2. What solutions does he offer in how the school could do better? Do you agree with his ideas?

"ENOUGH IS ENOUGH" BY ALANA BAUM, FROM *OTHERWORDS*, FEBRUARY 13, 2013

I've had enough.

Enough of rape being subject to terms like "legitimate."

Enough of hearing that my peers just "raped" their final exams.

Enough of being labeled too-politically-correct when I challenge the oversimplification and distortion of a word that is a dark reality for one in six American women.

Enough of having to explain that rape is not just a *Law & Order: SVU* scenario where a woman is held at gunpoint in a back alley.

And enough of hearing the stories of women I know that are survivors of back-alley rapes.

Enough of the GOP's attempts to prevent the reauthorization of the Violence Against Women Act, which, among other things, adds further protections for Native American women. Although this measure passed in the Senate on Tuesday, VAWA will face a tougher battle in the House.

One of the bill's main adversaries is Sen. Chuck Grassley (R-IA). He was among the 22 Republican Senators who voted against the measure. Grassley says it would threaten the "constitutional rights of defendants who would be tried in these tribal courts." What about the constitutional rights of Native American women who are 2.5 times more likely to be raped than any other demographic group in the United States?

And, more than anything, I've had enough of the horrific cases of violent sexual assault that continue to threaten the lives of women all around the world.

Last week in Acapulco, a group of armed, masked gunmen raped six Spanish women on vacation in Mexico.

In December, a 23-year-old woman was gang raped on a moving bus in Delhi in an attack so brutal that she later died.

According to national statistics, two women are sexually assaulted in India every hour. And these are just the reported crimes. A number of roadblocks stand in the way of justice: unrecorded medical evidence following cases of sexual assault, police that disregard rape complaints, and the vile suggestion that women marry their rapists in order to preserve their "honor."

And stories are still surfacing about the rampant sexual attacks that took place in Tahrir Square during the early days of Egypt's revolution and are continuing to take place at protests in Cairo.

On January 25, "the square witnessed nineteen cases of assault, including six in which women sustained knife wounds requiring medical care," writes Heba Saleh, the Cairo correspondent for the *Financial Times*. While Egyptian feminist groups and allies are seeking to raise awareness and secure protective measures, public figures are reinforcing the problem. Salafi preacher Ahmad Mahmoud Abdullah said last week that female activists show up to protests because they want to be raped.

These atrocities have gained enough media attention to stir our global consciousness from slumber. But they also speak to an epidemic of violence that runs much deeper.

Tomorrow is Valentine's Day. But it's also V-Day, a day of global mobilization to end violence against women and girls everywhere.

There will be strikes, rallies, protests, and flash mobs tomorrow in cities all around the world. I ask that you join me in standing up to demand an end to this brutality.

This isn't just a cause for women. Nor can it afford to be. This cause must lead to action not only by women, but by men. Not only by survivors of sexual assault, but by allies. Not only by the young, but by the old. Not only by college students, or feminists, or members of Congress, or religious leaders, but everyone. Neither the problem of violence against women — nor its potential solutions — will be apparent until we take collective action.

I've had enough. If you've also had enough, it's time to let the world know.

1. According to the author, what role does society play in normalizing sexual violence?

2. By speaking out against these issues, what can individuals accomplish?

"BYSTANDERS OFTEN DON'T INTERVENE IN SEXUAL HARASSMENT – BUT SHOULD THEY?" BY BIANCA FILEBORN, FROM *THE CONVERSATION* WITH THE PARTNERSHIP OF UNSW SYDNEY, FEBRUARY 20, 2017

As the summer music festival season winds down, there has been much reflection on the spate of sexual harassment and assaults at festivals this year. In one such piece, published in The Guardian, the author lamented the fact that no other punters stepped in when his female friend was harassed and assaulted in full view of others.

This lack of response is unsurprising. Bystanders are those who witness an event – sexual harassment and assault in this instance – and can choose to either ignore it or intervene in a way that aims to make a positive difference.

This unwillingness to intervene was reaffirmed in my own recent research on street harassment in Melbourne, where only a minority of participants had ever had someone else step in, despite the highly public nature of this behaviour.

Why don't people intervene when they witness sexual harassment and assault? And, more importantly, should they?

WHY DON'T PEOPLE INTERVENE?

Barriers to bystander intervention have been well documented.

In order to intervene, bystanders need to be able to recognise sexual harassment or assault when it is happening. A significant proportion of the population adheres to a range of problematic beliefs and stereotypes about sexual violence and violence against women, so it is questionable whether many people recognise incidents of sexual harassment or assault when they occur.

Even if bystanders do recognise that sexual harassment is occurring, they may not know what to do and lack confidence to intervene effectively. Bystanders can fear social embarrassment and breaching social norms. We know that the propensity to intervene is mediated by gender, with women generally more likely or more confident to intervene than men. One reason for this is that men are more likely to adhere to the aforementioned myths and misconceptions about sexual violence.

Diffusion of responsibility is perhaps the most commonly documented barrier to acting as a bystander. It is the "can't someone else do it?" of bystander intervention. If there are many witnesses to an act of harassment or assault, it can be unclear who should step in. Onlookers may simply assume that someone else will take action.

SHOULD BYSTANDERS INTERVENE?

We know that people often don't intervene and some of the reasons why they don't. But *should* bystanders intervene?

Bystander intervention is now a key component of many sexual violence prevention and sexual ethics programs. There are sound reasons for this. Bystander intervention seeks to shift responsibility for preventing sexual violence from victim/survivors to the broader community. Preventing sexual violence, and challenging the social and cultural attitudes that condone and facilitate it, is everybody's responsibility.

There is certainly some evidence to suggest that bystander education programs help to change attitudes towards sexual violence and increase the propensity for individuals to act as bystanders. Bystander education has also been associated with decreased rates of sexual assault on some US college campuses.

However, there are also a number of gaps in our knowledge that raise serious questions about whether, when, and how bystanders should intervene.

We know surprisingly little about bystander intervention "in action." For example, the impacts and outcomes of different types of bystander intervention remain largely unexamined. What "types" of bystander intervention are effective, and in which contexts? Do all forms of intervention have a positive impact, or are there sometimes unexpected or negative consequences?

Emerging evidence from my own research on street harassment suggests that bystanders can be at risk of harm when they intervene.

Although bystander intervention could sometimes effectively defuse an incident of harassment, some participants reported that having a bystander intervene didn't stop the harassment, could escalate the intensity of harassment, or simply displaced the harassment onto the bystander.

For example, when one participant's friend intervened in an incident of harassment, the perpetrator punched her friend in the face. In another case, a perpetrator screamed at a participant's partner and 'threatened to kill him' after he intervened in an assault.

Notably, this was often the case when the bystander directly confronted a perpetrator who was a stranger – it's less clear that this is an issue when calling out your mates on their sexist or harassing behaviour.

The risk of escalation or displacement raises the question of whether encouraging bystander intervention is ethical, and in what circumstances? As Moira Carmody has argued, "[E]thical bystander intervention requires the bystander to be mindful of caring for themselves, as well as the impact on the other person." If there is a perceived risk of escalation or physical violence, bystanders are well within their right not to intervene.

There is a clear need to establish further the circumstances in which bystander intervention is effective and to identify risk factors for escalation.

WHAT CAN BYSTANDERS DO?

This is not intended to let bystanders off the hook when it comes to intervening in, or preventing, sexual violence.

Findings from my study suggest that it is not always appropriate to intervene by confronting the perpetrator of harassment. But there are other strategies they can use, including:

- Calling police or security, or alerting staff to an incident.
- Asking the person being harassed if they're OK. Is there anything you can do to help them? It is important to listen to victims and what they want.
- Striking up a conversation with the person being harassed.
- If you feel safe to do so, taking photos or video of the perpetrator.
- Trying to create space to get the person being harassed away from the perpetrator. Can you help them move to a different seat on the train, for example?
- Talking to your friends about harassment and assault and calling them out if you see or hear them condoning or engaging in inappropriate behaviour.
- Educating yourself on what harassment and assault are and learning about different strategies for being a bystander.

Preventing sexual violence is everybody's responsibility, but we need to think carefully about how we do it.

1. What are a few reasons bystanders might not want to get involved in harassment incidents?

2. Do you think the actions suggested by the author are reasonable? Why or why not?

"THROUGH MY LOOKING GLASS" BY STELLA JAMES, FROM THE *JOURNAL OF INDIAN LAW AND SOCIETY*, NOVEMBER 6, 2013

Sometimes the most difficult things to write about are also the most essential. I feel this is especially true when many people, much more scholarly than [your]self, have already said and written a lot around the issue, and yet your own experience does not seem to fit into the wide net that they've cast. Gandhi once said "I have something far more powerful than arguments, namely, experience." And it is from these words that I derive what I consider the 'value' of this piece – not my experience per se, but from what I feel that my experience can tell us about much discussed issues in the country today.

Last December was momentous for the feminist movement in [this] country – almost an entire population seemed to rise up spontaneously against the violence [against] women and the injustices of a seemingly apathetic government. In the strange irony of situations that our world is replete with, the protests were the backdrop of my own experience. In Delhi at that time, interning during the winter vacations of my final year in University, I dodged police barricades and fatigue to go to the assistance of a highly reputed, recently retired Supreme Court judge whom I was working under during my penultimate semester. For my supposed diligence, I was rewarded with sexual assault (not physically injurious, but nevertheless violating) from a man old enough to be my grandfather. I won't go into the gory details, but suffice it to say that long after I'd left the room, the memory remained, in fact, still remains, with me.

So what bothered me about this incident? As a conditioned member of society, I had quickly "gotten over" the incident. But [that was] what worried me: that I had accepted what was essentially an 'unacceptable' situation. The more I thought about it, the more I realized that the crux of my unease lay in my inability to find a frame in which to talk, or even *think*, about my experience. While the incident affected me deeply, I felt little anger and almost no rancour towards the man; instead I was shocked and hurt that someone I respected so much would do something like this. My strongest reaction, really, was overwhelming sadness. But this sort of response was new to me. That I could understand his actions and forgive him for them, or that I could continue to think of him as an essentially "good" person, seemed a naïve position that [was] completely at odds with what I had come to accept was the "right" reaction to such incidents.

This emotional response was also completely at odds with the powerful feelings of righteous anger that the protestors in Delhi displayed. I am not trying to say that anger at the violence that women face is not a just or true response, but the polarization of women's rights debates in India, along with their intense emotionality, left me feeling that my only options were to either strongly condemn the judge or to betray my feminist principles. Perhaps this confusion came out of an inadequate understanding of feminist literature, but if so, isn't then my skewed perception a failing of feminism itself? If the shared experiences of women cannot be easily understood through a feminist lens, then clearly there is a cognitive vacuum that feminism fails to fill. Feminists talk of the guilt a woman faces when sexually harassed, like it is *her* fault. I felt a similar guilt, except my guilt wasn't at being assaulted, but at not reacting more strongly than I did. The very perspective that was meant to help me make sense of my experiences as a woman was the one that obscured the resolution of the problem in my own mind, presumably an effect that feminism does not desire. And if not a result of feminist theory itself, the form that it has taken in India, especially after recent incidents of sexual assault, strengthened the feeling of "[i[f you're not with us, you're against us" in a fight that I feel I can no longer take sides in.

All the talk during that time was of stricter punishment [and] of baying for the blood of "creepy" men. Five years of law school had taught me to look to the law for all solutions – even where I knew that the law was hopelessly inadequate – and my reluctance to wage a legal battle against the judge left me feeling cowardly. On reflection, though, I cannot help but wonder why I should have felt that way. As mentioned earlier, I bore, and still bear, no real ill-will towards the man and had no desire to put his life's work and reputation in question. On the other hand, I felt I had a responsibility to ensure that other young girls were not put in a similar situation. But I have been unable to find a solution that allows that. Despite the heated public debates, despite a vast army of feminist vigilantes, despite new criminal laws and sexual harassment laws, I have not found closure. The lack of such an alternative led to my facing a crippling sense of intellectual and moral helplessness.

The incident is now a while behind me, and they say time heals all wounds. But during the most difficult emotional times, what helped me most was the "insensitivity" of a close friend whose light-hearted mocking allowed me to *laugh* at an incident (and a man) that had caused me so much pain. Allowing myself to feel more than just anger at a man who violated me, something that I had never done before, is liberating! So, I want to ask you to think of one thing alone – when dealing with sexual violence, can we allow ourselves to embrace feelings beyond or besides anger and to accept the complexity of emotions that we face when dealing with *any* traumatic experience?

1. What is the author's experience with sexual harassment and gender violence?

2. Why does she not feel closure after the public outcry against sexual assault?

CONCLUSION

Sexual harassment and gender violence can take many shapes. It can be abuse by a partner or spouse, unwanted attention in the workplace, or violation in public. It can be emotional, mental, sexual, physical, or a combination of them all. What is true of all cases of gender violence and sexual harassment, whether against men or women, is that it has an insidious and far-reaching impact on the individuals to whom it occurs and for the society in which it takes place.

Our understanding of gender-based violence and sexual harassment has changed a great deal in recent decades, thanks in no small part to the tireless efforts of lawmakers and advocates who have dedicated their lives to passing laws that criminalize damaging and dangerous behaviors. We are also learning more and more about how men and women are both victims of harassment and how best we can talk about these issues so everyone feels they have a voice in the conversation. From the Civil Rights Act of 1964 to the Violence Against Women Act reauthorization of 2013, the laws that govern these issues have shown a gradual progression toward a society that does not accept behavior rooted in gender-based harassment.

There are many reasons why doing so is important. As the articles in this collection show, the impact of sexual harassment and gender violence is far reaching. These are issues around the world, shaped by events like war or disaster. The international community has worked hard to change perceptions of gender and how it impacts the acceptance of violence against certain parts of society, but we are still understanding what these issues mean on both a national and personal level. It shapes the workplace and the home and can negatively impact the overall economy of a country. It creates long-term emotional distress that can leave people unable to pursue their goals and can lead to discrimination against women. Ending sexual harassment and gender violence is not just about protecting individuals but is also about moving society as a whole forward.

Although there is still a long way to go before these issues are fully erased from our country, we have come far in a short amount of time. Today the debates about sexual harassment and gender violence are far removed from the days when it wasn't believed to be an issue at all. Instead, we are left to find the best ways to combat it and help its victims, which are questions we will likely be asking for years to come.

BIBLIOGRAPHY

Anderlini, Sanam Naraghi. "WDR Gender Background Paper." *World Bank*, February 19, 2010. https://openknowledge.world-bank.org/handle/10986/9250.

Baum, Alana. "Enough is Enough." *OtherWords*, February 13, 2013. https://otherwords.org/enough-rape-already.

Biden, Joe. "It's On Us to Stop Campus Sexual Assault." *White House Archives*, November 9, 2015. https://obamawhitehouse.archives.gov/the-press-office/2015/11/09/vice-president-joe-biden-op-ed-its-us-stop-campus-sexual-assault.

Brown, Brandon. "Appeals Court Slashes Award Against ASARCO in Sexual Harassment Case." *Cronkite News*, October 24, 2013. http://cronkitenewsonline.com/2013/10/appeals-court-slashes-award-against-asarco-in-sexual-harassment-case.

Cruz, Caitlin and Asha Anchan. "Government Slow to Respond to Epidemic of Sexual Assaults." *News21*, August 24, 2013. http://backhome.news21.com/article/mst.

Eisen, Michael. "Berkley's Handling of Sexual Harassment is a Disgrace." *It Is NOT Junk*, March 10, 2016. http://www.michaeleisen.org/blog/?p=1878.

Elba, Miriam. "New Documentary Uses Art to Resist Sexual Harassment in Egypt." *Waging Nonviolence*, October 8, 2014. http://wagingnonviolence.org/2014/10/new-documentary-uses-art-resist-sexual-harassment-egypt.

Fileborn, Bianca. "Bystanders Often Don't Intervene in Sexual Harassment -- But Should They?" *The Conversation*, February 20, 2017. https://theconversation.com/bystanders-often-dont-intervene-in-sexual-harassment-but-should-they-72794.

Lagos Lira, Claudia Paola and Patsili Toledo. "The Media and Gender-Based Murders of Women: Notes on the Cases in Europe and Latin America." *Heinrich Böll Foundation*, July 2014. https://eu.boell.org/en/2014/07/24/media-and-gender-based-murders-women-notes-cases-europe-and-latin-america.

Lake, Robert. "The Violence Against Women Reauthorization Act of 2013 Summary of Substantive Changes." *Michigan Poverty Law Program*, August 12, 2013. http://www.mplp.org/Newsletters/summer_2013_mplp_newsletter/the_violence_against_women_reauthorization_act_of_2013_summary_of_substantive_changes.

Law, Victoria. "Changing the Culture of Domestic Violence One Quilt Square at a Time." *Waging Nonviolence*, January 26, 2015. http://wagingnonviolence.org/feature/changing-culture-domestic-violence-one-quilt-square-time.

Law, Victoria. "What Are Men Doing to Challenge and Stop Gender Violence?" *Waging Nonviolence*, November 5, 2014. http://wagingnonviolence.org/feature/challenge-men-challenge-stop-gender-violence.

Liles, Laurie. "Chiapas Women Work Toward a 'Life Free of Violence'." *Cronkite Borderlands Project*, September 25, 2014. https://cronkite.asu.edu/buffett/chiapas/chiapas-women-work-toward-a-life-free-of-violence.

McCain, John. "Remarks by Senator John McCain on the Imaginary 'War on Women' on the Floor of the US Senate." *John McCain: US Senator*, April 26, 2012. https://www.mccain.senate.gov/public/index.cfm/floor-statements?ID=EF1B1995-C206-18CE-BDB1-89CD95F12F64.

Murray, Sarah. "International Guide to Addressing Gender-Based Violence Through Sport." *Women Win.* Retrieved March 22, 2017. http://guides.womenwin.org/gbv.

Planty, Michael and Lynn Langton, et al. "Female Victims of Sexual Violence, 1994-2010." *US Department of Justice*, May 31, 2016. https://www.bjs.gov/content/pub/pdf/fvsv9410.pdf.

Staff. *Booth v Hvass. United States Court of Appeals for the Eighth Circuit*, September 11, 2002. http://media.ca8.uscourts.gov/opndir/02/09/013210P.pdf.

Staff. *Meritor Savings Bank v. Vinson, (1986) No. 84-1979. United States Supreme Court*, June 19, 1986.

Staff. "Remarks by the President and Vice President at an Event for the Council on Women and Girls." *White House Archives*, January 22, 2014. https://obamawhitehouse.archives.gov/the-press-office/2014/01/22/remarks-president-and-vice-president-event-council-women-and-girls.

Stella, James. "Through My Looking Glass." *Journal of Indian Law and Society*, November 6, 2013. https://jilsblognujs.wordpress.com/2013/11/06/through-my-looking-glass.

Torres, Diana Anahi. "The Visa Curse." *OtherWords*, December 30, 2014. http://otherwords.org/the-visa-curse.

CHAPTER NOTES

INTRODUCTION

1. Cohen, Sascha. "A Brief History of Sexual Harassment in America Before Anita Hill." *Time*, April 11, 2016. http://time.com/4286575/sexual-harassment-before-anita-hill.

2. National Coalition Against Domestic Violence. "National Statistics." Retrieved March 29, 2017. http://ncadv.org/learn-more/statistics.

3. RAINN. "The Criminal Justice System: Statistics." Retrieved March 29, 2017. https://www.rainn.org/statistics/criminal-justice-system.

CHAPTER 1: WHAT ACADEMICS, EXPERTS, AND RESEARCHERS SAY

EXCERPT FROM "THE WORLD DEVELOPMENT REPORT GENDER BACKGROUND PAPER," BY SANAM NARAGHI ANDERLINI

i. Danish Ministry of Foreign Affairs, Warburton Mission II Report: EC Investigative Mission into the Treatment of Muslim Women in the Former Yugoslavia, 1993. Available at http://www.womenaid.org/press/info/humanrights/warburtonfull.htm#Scale%20of%20the%20problem

ii. http://www.ncjrs.gov/html/ojjdp/186162/page6.html

iii. Nepal Film Women Rebels, Sri Lanka personal communication UNICEF child protection adviser

iv. http://www.unhchr.ch/Huridocda/Huridoca.nsf/0/3d25270b-5fa3ea998025665f0032f220?Opendocumen

v. Carballo, M., Bryan Heal and Gabriela Horbarty, "Impact of Tsunami on Psycho-social Health", International Review of Psychiatry, June 2006; 18 (3): 217-233. http://www.icmh.ch/WebPDF/2006/2006-001-%20Article%20Int.%20Review%20of%20Psychiatry%20on%20Tsunami/CIRP_AB_165561.pdf

vi. Rwandan Ministry of Social Affairs, 2007 census estimates the number to be 309,368 (http://www.hirondellenews.com/content/view/2328/182/). IBUKA (the umbrella body of survivors' organizations in Rwanda) estimates the number to be nearer to 400,000.

vii. Karabegovic, D. "Bosnia Struggle to Overcome Male Rape Taboo", TRI issue 642, 16 April 2010, IWPR http://www.iwpr.net/report-news/bosnia-struggle-overcome-male-rape-taboo

viii. http://www.who.int/gender/en/infobulletinconflict.pdf

ix. UNIFEM, *Voicing the Needs of Women and Men in Gaza: Beyond the Aftermath of the 23-Day Israeli Military Operations*, UNIFEM: United Nations, New York 2009.

x. Sex Traffickers Target Women in War-Torn Iraq Report, IRIN, 26 October 2006 xi Goode, E. After Combat, Victims of an Inner War (New York Times, August 1, 2009). http://www.nytimes.com/2009/08/02/us/02suicide.html?ref=posttraumaticstressdisorder

xi. Goode, E. After Combat, Victims of an Inner War (New York Times, August 1, 2009).http://www.nytimes.com/2009/08/02/us/02suicide.html?ref=posttraumaticstressdisorder

xii. "Afghanistan: UN Official Urges Steps to Prevent Child Deaths in Conflict", Irinnews, 24 February 2010. http://www.un.org/apps/news/story.asp?NewsID=33879&Cr=afghan&Cr1

xiii. Castillo Diaz, P. and Leticia Anderson, Guinea-Conakry: the price of political rape", OpenDemocracy, 10 February 2010, http://www.opendemocracy.net/5050/pablo-castillo-diaz-letitia-anderson/guinea-conakryprice-of-political-rape

xiv. IRIN, 'DRC: Sexual Violence Prevention and Reintegration Funding "falls through cracks" http://www.alertnet.org/the-news/newsdesk/IRIN/d60a2e98dba1c8474547947c407c73a6.htm

xv. http://www.huffingtonpost.com/zainab-salbi/preventing-and-addressing_b_333792.html

CHAPTER 3: WHAT THE COURTS SAY

EXCERPT FROM "UNITED STATES SUPREME COURT: *MERITOR SAVINGS BANK V. VINSON,* (1986) NO. 84-1979" FROM THE UNITED STATES SUPREME COURT

[Footnote 1] The remedial provisions of Title VII were largely modeled on those of the National Labor Relations Act (NLRA). See Albemarle Paper Co. v. Moody, 422 U.S. 405, 419, and n. 11 (1975); see also Franks v. Bowman Transportation Co., 424 U.S. 747, 768 -770 (1976).

[Footnote 2] For NLRA cases, see, e. g., Graves Trucking, Inc. v. NLRB, 692 F.2d 470 (CA7 1982); NLRB v. Kaiser Agricultural Chemical, Division of Kaiser Aluminum & Chemical Corp., 473 F.2d 374, 384 (CA5 1973); Amalgamated Clothing Workers of America v. NLRB, 124 U.S. App. D.C. 365, 377, 365 F.2d 898, 909 (1966).[477 U.S. 57, 79]

EXCERPT FROM *SCOTT BOOTH V. SHERYL RAMSTAD HVASS,* UNITED STATES COURT OF APPEALS FOR THE EIGHTH CIRCUIT

1. Appellee Charles Weaver, the Commissioner of the Department of Public Safety, administers the domestic abuse statutes through a division of the Department of Public Safety: the Center for Crime Victim Services ("the Center"). Under sections 611A.31-.361 of the domestic abuse statutes, the Center provides grants of state and federal funds to programs that assist battered women and domestic abuse victims. Under sections 611A.37-.375, the Center also makes per diem payments to various shelters to reimburse the shelters for costs of providing their clients with food, lodging, and safety.

2. Domestic Abuse Project, Central Minnesota Task Force on Battered Women, and Lakes Crises Center, all organizations that

provide services to victims of domestic violence and receive funding through the domestic abuse statutes, moved to intervene in the lawsuit. Magistrate Judge Jonathan G. Lebedoff granted that motion.

3. The Honorable Michael J. Davis, United States District Judge for the District of Minnesota.

4. In the district court, the appellants also alleged general standing to bring their case in federal court. The district court held that the appellants failed to allege a direct injury. The appellants do not make a general standing argument on appeal.

CHAPTER 4: WHAT ADVOCACY ORGANIZATIONS SAY

EXCERPT FROM THE "INTERNATIONAL GUIDE TO ADDRESSING GENDER-BASED VIOLENCE THROUGH SPORT," BY SARA MURRAY

7. *Koss, M. (1990). The women's mental health research agenda: violence against women. American Psychologist, 45: 374-380 Retrieved from http://www.scielo.br/scielo.php?pid=S0102-311X1994000500009&script=sci_a...*

8. *Koss, MP, The under-detection of rape: methodological choices influence incidence estimates, J. Soc. Issues, 1992, Vol. 48, p61-75*

9. *Bunch, C. and Carrillo, R. (1992). Gender Violence: A Development and Human Rights Issue, Atti Press, Dublin.*

10. *Retrieved from http://www.unfpa.org/webdav/site/global/shared/documents/publications/20...*

11. *Bensley LS, Van Eenwyk J, Simmons KW, "Self-reported childhood sexual and physical abuse and adult HIV risk behaviours and heavy drinking", Am J. Prev. Med. 2000, 18(2), 151-8. The report concluded that "one third to one half of those reporting HIV-risk behaviours in a general-population survey also reported childhood abuse".*

12. *Boyer & Fine, 1992; Zierler et al., 1991; Finkelhor, 1987; Cassese, 1993; Paone & Chavkin, 1993*

13. *Centers for Disease Control and Prevention (CDC). Costs of intimate partner violence against women in the United States. Atlanta (GA): CDC, National Center for Injury Prevention and Control; 2003. Retrieved from http://www.cdc.gov/violenceprevention/pdf/IPV-Book-a.pdf*

14. *"A/RES/48/104. Declaration on the Elimination of Violence against Women"(1993). Retrieved from http://www.un.org/documents/ga/res/48/a48r104.htm*

15. *Kimmel, M.S. (2002). Gender Symmetry in Domestic Violence: A Substantive and Methodological Research Review. Violence Against Women, 8, 1332-1363. Retrieved from http://www.ncjrs.gov/App/Publications/abstract.aspx?ID=198004*

16. *http://www.domesticabuseproject.org/*

17. *http://www.ifad.org/gender/glossary.htm*

18. *Caputi, J. & Russell, D. E. H. (1992). Femicide: Sexist Terrorism against Women. In Femicide: The Politics of Woman-Killing. Edited by Jane Caputi and Diana E.H. Russell. Twayne Publishers: New York*

19. *UN Women (n.d.) Gender, In Concepts and definitions. Retrieved from http://www.un.org/womenwatch/osagi/conceptsandefinitions.htm*

20. *http://www.un.org/womenwatch/daw/cedaw/*

21. *http://www.un.org/womenwatch/osagi/conceptsandefinitions.htm*

22. *http://en.wikipedia.org/wiki/Gender_roles*

23. *Amnesty International (n.d.) Human rights basics. Retrieved from www.amnestyusa.org*

24. *Infanticide (n.d.) In The Free Dictionary. Retrieved from http://encyclopedia2.thefreedictionary.com/Infanticide+(humans)*

25. *Post exposure prophylaxis (n.d.). In Wikipediahttp://en.wikipedia. org/wiki/Post-exposure_prophylaxis*

26. *Uend Poverty (n.d.). UN Chronicle. Retrieved from http://www. uend.org/blog/2010/01/11/poverty-potential-definitions/*

27. *Power (n.d.). In Merriam-Webster's online dictionary (11th ed.) Retrieved from http://www.m-w.com/dictionary/power*

28. *UNDAW (n.d.). General recommendations made by the Committee on the Elimination of Discrimination against Women. Retrieved from http://www.un.org/womenwatch/daw/cedaw/recommendations/recomm.htm*

29. *Jing, W. (n.d.) Gender Stereotypes. Retrieved from http://guilford-journals.com/doi/abs/10.1521/soco.2015.33.4.1?journalCode=soco*

30. *Helium (n.d.). What is systematic rape? Retrieved from http://www. crimesofwar.org/a-z-guide/sexual-violence-systematic-rape/*

31. *World Health Organisation (n.d.). Violence. Retrieved from http:// www.who.int/topics/violence/en/*

"THE VIOLENCE AGAINST WOMEN REAUTHORIZATION ACT OF 2013 SUMMARY OF SUBSTANTIVE CHANGES" BY ROBERT LAKE

1. Violence Against Women Act, Pub. L. No. 103-322, tit. IV, 108 Stat. 1902 (1994) (codified as amended in scattered sections of 8, 16, 18, 28, and 42 U.S.C.).

2. While women victims are the primary focus of the act, Senator Joe Biden, author of VAWA, explains that men are protected as well: "The reality is that the vast majority of victims of domestic violence are women and children, and most outreach organizations take those demographics into consideration when providing services . . . The bottom line is - violence is violence no matter what gender the victim. Because of that, the Violence Against Women Act applies to all victims of domestic violence, irrespective of their gender. Nothing in the act denies

services, programs, funding or assistance to male victims of violence." Robin Brown, "Billboards criticize Biden's violence law," *The News Journal* (April 29, 2005).

3. The Violence Against Women Reauthorization Act of 2013, Pub. L. No. 113-4 (2013), *available at* http://www.gpo.gov/fdsys/pkg/BILLS-113s47enr/pdf/BILLS-113s47enr.pdf.

4. Black, M.C., Basile, K.C., Breiding, M.J., Smith, S.G., Walters, M.L., Merrick, M.T., Chen, J., & Stevens, M.R., National Center for Injury Prevention and Control, Centers for Disease Control and Prevention, *The National Intimate Partner and Sexual Violence Survey (NISVS): 2010 Summary Report* 18 (2011), *available at* http://www.cdc.gov/ViolencePrevention/pdf/NISVS_Report2010-a.pdf.

5. Office on Violence Against Women, U.S. Dep't of Justice, *2012 Biennial Report to Congress on the Effectiveness of Grant Programs Under the Violence Against Women Act* 5 (2012), *available at* http://www.ovw.usdoj.gov/docs/2012-biennial-report-to-congress.pdf.

6. *Id*.

7. VAWA 2013 defines "youth" as a person who is 11-24 years old. Previous iterations of VAWA referred to a person in this age group as a "teen" or "young adult."

8. *Id.* at 6.

9. Black et al. at 18.

10. *Id.* at 5.

11. *Id.* at 1.

12. *Id.* at 19.

13. *2012 Biennial Report to Congress* at 8.

14. Broken down by type of offense, "grantees in 13 of VAWA's discretionary grant programs provided services to an average

of 6,748 victims/survivors of sexual assault, 115,733 victims/survivors of domestic violence/dating violence, and 2,567 victims/survivors of stalking." *Id.* at 9.

15. *Id.* at 15-16.

16. *Id* at 29-30.

17. Catalano, Shannan M., Bureau of Justice Statistics, U.S. Dep't of Justice, *Intimate Partner Violence, 1993-2010* (2012), *available at* http://www.bjs.gov/content/pub/pdf/ipv9310.pdf.

18. Pickert, Kate, *What's Wrong with the Violence Against Women Act?*, Time Magazine, Feb. 27, 2013, *available at* http://nation.time.com/2013/02/27/whats-wrong-with-the-violence-against-women-act/.

19. Clark, K. A, Biddle, A., & Martin, S., *A cost-benefit analysis of the Violence Against Women Act of 1994*, Violence Against Women, 8(4), 417-428 (2002).

20. Logan, T., Walker, R., Hoyt, W., & Faragher, T., U.S. Dep't of Justice *The Kentucky civil protective order study: A rural and urban multiple perspective study of protective order violation consequences, responses, and costs* (No. NCJRS 228350) (2009).

21. Press Release, Office of Public Affairs, U.S. Dep't of Justice, Statement by Attorney General Eric Holder on the House Passage of the Reauthorization of the Violence Against Women Act (Feb. 28, 2013), *available at* http://www.justice.gov/opa/pr/2013/February/13-ag-253.html.

22. Congressional Budget Office, *CBO Cost Estimate for S.47, The Violence Against Women Reauthorization Act of 2013, as Published in Rules Committee Print 113-2* (Feb. 27, 2013), *available at* http://www.cbo.gov/sites/default/files/cbofiles/attachments/VAWAtable_Rules.pdf.

23. Stegman, Erik, Center for American Progress, *3 Reasons the Violence Against Women Act Has Been Bipartisan for 18 Years, and Why Congress Should Fast Track It* (Jan. 23, 2013), *available at* http://www.americanprogress.org/issues/women/

news/2013/01/23/50438/3-reasons-the-violence-against-women-act-has-been-bipartisan-for-18-years-and-why-congress-should-fast-track-it/.

24. Press Release, The Senate Judiciary Committee Majority Staff, The Violence Against Women Reauthorization Act: Renewing the Commitment to Protect All Victims of Violence (2013), *available at* http://www.leahy.senate.gov/imo/media/doc/042512VAWA-GeneralOverview-OnePager.pdf.

25. *2012 Biennial Report to Congress* at 9.

26. Letter from Laura W. Murphy & Vania Leveille, The American Civil Liberties Union, to Members of the House of Representatives (Feb. 27, 2013), *available at* http://www.aclu.org/files/assets/aclu_letter_on_house_substitute_amendment_to_vawa_2013-_final.pdf (citation omitted).

27. *2012 Biennial Report to Congress* at 85.

28. *2012 Biennial Report to Congress* at 8.

29. Hon. David J. Hickton, United States Attorney for the Western District of Pennsylvania, Remarks at Washington County's Crime Victims' Rights Week Observance (Apr. 23, 2013), *available at* http://www.justice.gov/usao/paw/djh_crime_victims_rights_week_remarks.html.

30. Letter from Laura W. Murphy, Director, ACLU Washington Legislative Office, to Members of the Senate (Feb. 7, 2013), *available at* http://www.aclu.org/files/assets/aclu_letter_re_vawa_grassley_substitute_2-7-13-final.pdf.

31. The National Coalition of Anti-Violence Programs, *Lesbian, Gay, Bisexual, Transgender, Queer and HIV-Affected Intimate Partner Violence* (2010), *available at* http://www.cuav.org/wp-content/uploads/2012/08/7243_2010IPVReport.pdf.

32. *2012 Biennial Report to Congress* at 99.

33 Letter from Laura W. Murphy & Vania Leveille, The American Civil Liberties Union, to Members of the House of

Representatives (Feb. 27, 2013), *available at* http://www.aclu. org/files/assets/aclu_letter_on_house_substitute_amend-ment_to_vawa_2013-_final.pdf (citation omitted).

34. 20 U.S.C. § 1092(f).

35. Memorandum from Lynn Mahaffie, Senior Director, Policy Coordination, Development and Accreditation Service, U.S. Dep't of Education, Implementation of Changes Made to the Clery Act by the Violence Against Women Reauthorization Act of 2013 (May 29, 2013), *available at* https://surveys.ope. ed.gov/security/images/Instructions/EA%20Clery%20and%20 VAWA%20final.pdf.

36. Tjaden, P. & Thoemes, N., The National Institute of Justice, U.S. Dep't of Justice, Full Report of the Prevalence, Incidence and Consequences of Violence Against Women (Nov. 2000), *available at* https://www.ncjrs.gov/pdffiles1/nij/183781.pdf.

37. Malcoe, L., Duran, B., & Montgomery, J., *Socioeconomic Disparities in Intimate Partner Violence Against Native American Women: A Cross-Sectional Study*, BMC Medicine 2:20 (2004) *available at* http://www.biomedcentral.com/1741-7015/2/20.

38. Letter from Laura W. Murphy & Vania Leveille, The American Civil Liberties Union, to Members of the House of Representatives (Feb. 27, 2013), *available at* http://www.aclu.org/files/assets/ aclu_letter_on_house_substitute_amendment_to_vawa_2013-_ final.pdf (citation omitted).

39. Letter from Ronald Weich, Assistant Attorney General, U.S. Dep't. of Justice, to Hon. Joseph R. Biden Jr., Vice President, (July 21, 2011), *available at* http://www.justice.gov/tribal/docs/ legislative-proposal-violence-against-native-women.pdf.

40. *Id*.

41. *Id*.

42. Tribal Justice and Safety, U.S. Dep't of Justice, *VAWA 2013*

and Tribal Jurisdiction Over Non-Indian Perpetrators of Domestic Violence 1 (2013), *available at* http://www.justice.gov/tribal/docs/vawa-2013-tribal-jurisdiction-overon-indian-perpetrators-domesticviolence.pdf.

43. "A tribe can start prosecuting non-Indian abusers sooner than March 7, 2015, if – [1] The tribe's criminal justice system fully protects defendants' rights under Federal law; [2] The tribe asks to participate in the new Pilot Project; and [3] The Justice Department grants the tribe's request and sets a starting date." *Id.*

GLOSSARY

communal Within a group and impacting that group as a whole.

consent Permission or agreement, which can be verbal or non-verbal.

domestic violence Aggression or abuse between partners or spouses.

emasculation A loss of masculinity, which is seen as negative or humiliating in many cultures.

female genital mutilation (FGM) A cultural practice in which part of the external reproductive system is removed as a rite of passage, causing extreme pain and possible infection.

femicide The targeted murder of women.

forced early marriage Usually arranged marriages made before one or both participants are at the age of consent and against the will of the minors.

gender inequality Disparities in resources or opportunities that occur between men and women in a society.

gender violence Aggression or abuse targeting an individual based on their gender.

human development The measure of the opportunity, freedom, and quality of life afforded to a country's citizens.

impunity A lack of consequences or being held accountable for an action that is harmful or illegal.

radicalization The process by which an individual is encouraged to accept an extreme ideology, which can include the advocating of violence against women or other marginalized groups.

sensationalization To present an event or situation in a way designed to lure in viewers or readers, which turns it into a public spectacle.

sexual assault Physical sexual contact that takes place without the consent of the recipient, including rape or fondling.

sexual harassment Inappropriate and unwanted physical or verbal attention in a professional or social setting.

structural violence Instances in which an institution or social structure, such as a government or norm, can be harmful to individuals.

taboo A norm or belief that makes certain behaviors frowned upon or forbidden within a society.

FOR MORE INFORMATION

BOOKS

Duramy, Benedetta Faedi. *Gender and Violence in Haiti*. New Brunswick, NJ: Rutgers University Press, 2014.

Factora-Borchers, Lisa. *Dear Sister: Letters From Survivors of Sexual Violence*. London, UK: AK Press, 2014.

Halbrook, Kristin. *Every Last Promise*. New York, NY: HarperTeen, 2015.

Hubbard, Jennifer. *Until It Hurts to Stop*. New York, NY: Viking Books for Young Readers, 2013.

Moser, Elise. *Lily and Taylor*. Toronto, CA: Groundwood Books, 2013.

Oliver, Kelly. *Hunting Girls: Sexual Violence from The Hunger Games to Campus Rape*. New York, NY: Columbia University Press, 2016.

Parker, S. M. *The Girl Who Fell*. New York, NY: Simon Pulse, 2016.

Smith, Andrea. *Conquest: Sexual Violence and American Indian Genocide*. Durham, NC: Duke University Press, 2015.

Thomas, Gillian. *Because of Sex: One Law, Ten Cases, and Fifty Years That Changed American Women's Lives at Work*. New York, NY: St Martin's Press, 2016.

Tripp, Aili Mari et al. *Gender, Violence, and Human Security*. New York, NY: NYU Press, 2013.

WEBSITES

CARE

www.care.org

CARE is a national nonprofit working around the world to end gender violence and achieve social justice. Its website provides information on global gender discrimination, avenues for advocacy, and ways to get involved.

The Rape, Abuse & Incest National Network (RAINN)

www.rainn.org

The website of the largest national organization fighting against sexual violence features statistics and other research into sexual assault, as well as advocacy information.

United Nations Women

www.unwomen.org

This international organization advocates around the world on behalf of women and other victims of gender violence. Its website includes news about current projects and a digital library documenting women's rights around the globe.

INDEX

ABOUT THE EDITOR

Bridey Heing is a writer and book critic based in Washington, DC. She holds degrees in political science and international affairs from DePaul University and Washington University in Saint Louis. Her areas of focus are comparative politics and Iranian politics. Her master's thesis explores the evolution of populist politics and democracy in Iran since 1900. She has written about Iranian affairs, women's rights, and art and politics for publications like the *Economist*, *Hyperallergic*, and the *Establishment*. She also writes about literature and film. She enjoys traveling, reading, and exploring Washington, DC's many museums.